The Dance of Teaching Childbirth Education

Essentials and Insights

Julie Jensen
Phd, LCCE, FACCE

Connie Livingston
BS, RN, LCCE, FACCE, ICCE, CMBE, IAT

Praeclarus Press, LLC

www.PraeclarusPress.com

Praeclarus Press, LLC
2504 Sweetgum Lane
Amarillo, Texas 79124 USA
806-367-9950
www.PraeclarusPress.com

DISCLAIMER

The information contained in this publication is advisory only and is not intended to replace sound clinical judgment or individualized patient care. The author disclaims all warranties, whether expressed or implied, including any warranty as the quality, accuracy, safety, or suitability of this information for any particular purpose.

ISBN: 978-1-946665-15-7
©2018 Julie Jensen and Connie Livingston. All rights reserved.

Cover Design: Ken Tackett
Developmental Editing: Kathleen Kendall-Tackett
Copy Editing: Chris Tackett
Layout & Design: Nelly Murariu

"It is noble to teach oneself, but still nobler to teach others—and less trouble."

— **Mark Twain**

CONTENTS

ACKNOWLEDGMENTS
AND DEDICATION

It would be impossible to duly give recognition to all the individuals in the past, and those in the present, who continue to promote and recognize birth for what it is: a normal, natural, miraculous process. Many of our wondrous predecessors are gone now, but we all benefit from their accomplishments, and will always continue to do so. Many of us have had astounding mentors who encouraged us to network, continue our birth work, and keep our strength in numbers by mentoring and training our valued childbirth education participants.

We want to continue and add to this powerful legacy, and thought it was time—more than time—to write this book. Although extremely helpful educational guides exist, we have not had a book published for birth professionals, by birth professionals, for quite some time. We want the work of our matriarchs and contemporaries to strongly continue and not fade. We have tremendous access to research studies, but no current books center on the heart and process of teaching. This labor of love is dedicated to the following people, for without them, there would be no book:

To the many andragogical learners in my classes, who have touched my heart and kept me going through the rewards and challenges, more than they will ever know.

To the endearing participants in training, and mentees who have entered my life and taught me much of what I know.

To my dear friend and colleague, Connie, who believed enough in me as a co-author, and gave me so much insight and acceptance in writing this book.

To my wonderful family and friends, who were all much less surprised than I ever was that I became a published author.

To my favorite four-legged, furry guy, Lazarus, who was such a good listener and patient companion through this process, who sadly succumbed to cancer during this journey.

To De, my colleague and friend, whom I have always greatly respected. I learned much from you in our journey from mentor/mentee to co-directors of our training program and the many steps in between. Thank you!

To Boni, who so graciously stepped in as the wonderful contributor, and has added so much.

And especially to my father, who continues to look down upon me with great belief and inspiration.

Thank you, Racheal, for all of your typing, patience, and edits!

FOREWORD

> "The keenness of our vision
> depends not on how much we can
> see, but on how much we feel."
> – Helen Keller

My contributions to this book are based on decades of teaching a variety of childbirth education classes, and training and managing educators. Educationally sound information, ideas, and strategies, integrated with evidence-based findings, relevance, and empowerment have been my focus.

I currently teach in hospital settings, coordinate and manage a hospital parent-education department, educate educators, and will always be a sharing, lifelong learner. I hold my doctorate in the impact of adult participatory learning behaviors. My life is still unfolding with this amazing privilege of teaching childbirth education.

It had truly been a wonder and adventure co-authoring with Connie, who was such an astonishingly bright, witty expert. We had so many conversations, and such quality networking, like birth-junkie neighbors who just happened to live over 1,200 miles apart. What's a little geographical distance when you had the best with which to work? After Connie passed away, it was a privilege to have Boni step in as a willing and intrinsic contributor.

I am trusting, and I believe Connie would have as well, that you, reader, will be enlightened about your teaching and yourself by this book, our "labor of love."

JULIE JENSEN

INTRODUCTION

One of the wisest women I never knew was the late Joan Erikson. She said, "[...] the most important thing is to share what you know. Be generative. Pass it on. That is what makes all the difference [...]." This is not only our gift, as authors, but our responsibility. We all want to carry the birth culture as individuals finding our souls within ourselves, and spreading the word with our hearts. We are the caretakers of the world.

If you are reading this book, thank you. Writing it has been such a labor of love. It started a few years ago when Connie had the idea of creating an edition of *Childbirth Education: Practice, Research, and Theory*, the last edition released in 2000. It was a compilation of chapters written by over 30 expert contributors, and so many of us treasured these beautiful pearls of wisdom. However, due to logistical challenges, Connie and I became the co-authors of this book, and we chose to include more strategies than content. I am fortunate and blessed that I was chosen. Connie and I met long ago (and again and again) in the exhibit halls of annual conferences. We had this connection, and would make each other smile. Those smiles soon turned into much laughter, as we saw humor in many things. This led to a wonderful professional and personal connection. The unexpected death of Connie during this whole process has been a tremendous loss on so many levels, but in memory and tribute to her, I knew the book must continue to completion. Her integral role as an educator, leader, author, and most of all, an inspiring friend, full of love and fun, created no doubt with this decision.

We bring that to you, along with a balance of numerous suggestions, evidence-based practices, and common sense in this wonderful field of childbirth education. We bring you our combined experience of more than 70 years in *The Dance of Teaching Childbirth Education: Essentials and Insights*. The math was easy to calculate, and the experience, unquantifiable. We both probably became addicted (in a good way, of course) to birth from the time each of us experienced our very own births.

Labor and birth is such a unique, intertwining process that is basic and natural, yet there is so much evidence-based information about almost every facet, and we are still able to help women empower themselves as we encourage them, repeatedly, to listen to their bodies. As childbirth educators, we consistently balance going from our head to our heart. We must stay on track with information, observe our group and individuals, while staying engaged and engaging. In addition, we provide a variety of activities to meet learning styles and interests, and, oh yes, stay within the timeframe. It is a miracle and true devotion that we maintain the passion that we do on the teeter-totter! In this balancing act and multitasking that is so vital, we combine evidence-based information with what is in our hearts. That can either feel conflicting, and, at times, affect the earnestness of our teaching, or it can be empowering. It is our choice. This book does not focus mostly on content. Rather, it offers you insights on your teaching and strategies, and helps you organize your curriculum.

Being a childbirth educator can be isolating. Yet we are one of the most sharing groups on the planet. It is vital that we stay connected through local gatherings and conferences rather than remaining isolated, sitting in front of our electronic devices. We sincerely hope that this book will not only help you individually, but be a networking tool for you as well.

Our combined 70 years of experience allowed us to evolve into the mentors we looked to for so many years. We realized we needed to write this book, leaving this legacy to our "birth and baby" peers. We thank you for your interest, and desire to be open and expand your horizons.

The Foundations of Childbirth Education

Historically, where did childbirth educators, as well as the improving, contemporary model of birth, come from? Not an easy question to answer. There are so many facets to the richness of this (our) history. Hopefully, the insights that are to follow will interest birth-related providers and educators to use in teaching our greatest beneficiaries. Our participants need to be aware that our curriculum is based on evidence.

Our foundation, however, goes much deeper. Women have been teaching and supporting others in birth since the beginning of time. Then, in the late 1800s or early 1900s, depending on the sources you consult, birth became a medical event in a hospital setting. This appeared to be for several legitimate reasons, such as the illusion of safety, the accessibility of equipment, and involvement of trained physicians. But there were some negative results when birth moved into the hospital. Providers were trained to treat patients in the hospital, viewing normal, natural birth as a pathological condition. Providers were blamed for changes. These changes caused women to not have control, which led to distressing birth memories for many women. However, generations of consumers accepted this and thought it was safer. This shift was not entirely the fault of the medical system. Consumers wanted it too. That was the medical culture and training for those times, but at what cost?

Educators also taught in ways we thought were best, and in how we were trained. Some examples:

- We were strongly advised to not even use the word "pain," but instead to use "discomfort."

- We thought just "total active relaxation," breathing, and laying on the bed was most effective.
- We thought just showing the Labor Chart would result in participants understanding labor (covered in Chapter 1).
- We were taught that "clumping" all medical procedures and interventions in one class would be most effective (covered in Chapter 1).
- We thought "practicing" relaxation, breathing, and massage for a bit at the end of class would suffice (covered in Chapter 1).

What were we thinking? As educators, we have come a long way in how we teach, just as the medical community has in their approaches with evidence-based practices and information. As educators, we are realizing what is best and most relevant medically for safe, healthy births. Many of you may have had expectant mothers attend class with their mothers who are thrilled with what we are now teaching, compared to what they were taught when preparing for birth.

The medical model has lasted quite a long time as birth interventions became the norm in many facilities. As guidelines shift, we now need to compare what patients thought was best and safest to what physicians are trained to do. The circle has been a large one, and is still making its way back to birth being a normal, natural experience. We all know of the huge strides that have been made, and that the circle is not complete in all areas categorically, as well as geographically. Empowerment, awareness of options, advocating for yourself, and being respected and consulted has significantly spread in medical settings. There are so many historical and contemporary advocates who have rocked the world of birth. To fully appreciate this circle and these strides is to start with early sources. Watch a YouTube video called *The Timeless Way*, and you may find it fascinating and appalling at the same time. Read *My Life in Birth* by Elisabeth Bing and Libby Colman, and *Thank you, Dr. Lamaze* by Marjorie Karmel to truly appreciate the strong foundation that advocates of normal birth laid. Listing them all would at least be equal to the size of a phonebook. Remember those?

Yes, our history includes questionable and frustrating prac-tices. Many hospitals in the country have created birthing suites: comfortable, relaxing environments with lighting, aromatherapy, tools, tubs, LDRP models, routine skin to skin for a time right after birth, rooming-in, elimination of Level One nurseries, and much more. Of course, every hospital does not have these, but these changes do entail a huge movement. Think of all the procedures that are no longer routine at many facilities, such as continuous monitoring for unmedicated birthing women, shaving, enemas, separation of mother and baby, supine pushing positions, and high rate of Second-Stage interventions. As will be discussed later, evidence-based information has changed the world of birth, as well as the American College of Obstetricians and Gynecologists' (ACOG's) Guidelines regarding dilation changing with phases of labor to allow low-risk laboring women to delay being in the hospital (*Nation's Ob-gyns Take Aim at Preventing Cesareans*), induc-tions (unless a medical necessity) not before 39 weeks, and the very recent ACOG's 2017 Committee Opinion, *Approaches to Limit Interventions During Labor and Birth*, which covers several areas. These are all accessible online, and educators and providers should seek them out to stay current. These guidelines reflect the efforts of many of the original and contemporary advocates, and all of those in between. More insight has allowed the birth field to positively impact labor and birth, and understand the improvements for all.

Long before evidence-based practice, birth advocate organiza-tions were formed and continue to increase our strength in childbirth education for individual and group networking. Lamaze International and ICEA (International Childbirth Education Association) were both formed in the early 60s with great visions, missions, goals, and position papers. (Interestingly, ACOG was formed in 1888.) Other organizations are listed in the Social Media section.

We are fortunate to have so many resources and professional organizations. As many of you know, we also have had the Six Healthy Birth Practices to guide us for a number of years: four were originally adapted from the World Health Organization (WHO) as evidence-based practices, and two were added by Lamaze International to become *The Lamaze® Healthy Birth Practices:*

- Let labor begin on its own.
- Walk, move around, and change positions throughout labor.
- Bring a loved one, friend, or doula for continuous support.
- Avoid interventions that are not medically necessary.
- Avoid giving birth on your back and follow your body's urges to push.
- Keep the mother and baby together – it's best for the mother, baby, and breastfeeding.

These have become routine in many, but not all, facilities. A document on the Lamaze.org website aligns these practices with ACOG positions.

Mentoring

Personal connections are another way to stay current in our information and teaching. This could be done in such a variety of ways. Whether you are new or experienced, find experienced educators who can mentor you. You can share ideas, questions, and concerns. This work can be isolating, yet we all have so much to share. I have learned so much from individuals at all levels of experience.

Even well-known educators have so much kindness, compassion, and care to offer. In 1994, when I was inducted as a FACCE (Fellow of the Academy of Certified Childbirth Educators) at our annual conference, we were called up and greeted individually by Elisabeth Bing. I thought "how wonderful," but gasped at the same time. Somehow, I found my legs, went up, and she looked right into my eyes, shook my hand, and said, "I am so very proud of you." I asked her if I should curtsy since she was royalty, and she thought, in her very humble and gracious way, that that was so funny. We became wonderful acquaintances after that. In 2002, when we were having a fundraiser at one of our conferences, and I was the hostess of a talkshow skit, I needed to recruit "guests" to interview. I called Elisabeth and explained what we were doing. She agreed, and then asked what the questions would be. I greatly appreciated her trust because they were funny questions that could have been challenging to answer, and she still agreed, at age 88! (Do not try and do the math; Elisabeth was still teaching into her late 80s, and I still have quite a ways to go.)

Another "superstar" who became a close friend and mentor was Donna Ewy Edwards. Those of us in Colorado were indeed very fortunate that she moved back to Colorado. She had published several books, planned, and organized teacher training programs in the United States, Mexico, and Europe. She brought organized childbirth education to Colorado, helped to start the Colorado Lamaze® Teacher Training Program, as well as our local chapter. I was at one of her local presentations and went up to her afterwards to share one of my stories. We connected and became very good friends for over 20 years until she passed away. She sponsored me in becoming a FACCE, and handed over the Teacher Training Program to me and another colleague. She offered such encouragement as I was completing my PhD (actually, she regularly cracked the whip for me to finish my dissertation, but I thought stating it as "encouragement" sounded more tactful). Find those mentors and helpful peers! We must carry on as advocates and work as a large team with peers, mentors (who become peers), leaders, providers, and the many others that are involved in our birth environments and areas. Our main focus is reaching our class participants. Ironically, the more the childbearing population uses technology, the more aware we are becoming in reducing technology with evidence-based practices to renew the normalcy of birth. A thrilling parallel! Keep moving forward, stay fresh, current, and full of passion and care. What are your motivators? How do you want to influence the parents you teach in the few hours you have with them? I recently received a class evaluation that included two very powerful and meaningful statements about the class: "Great summary of birthing process and relaxation techniques," and "I feel like I know what to expect now. I feel even less fearful about the process and empowered." Wow, I do not think I could have written my Class Goals any better!

There is a common saying that you are not your occupation. That does not hold true for childbirth educators. We are what we do or we would not be able to do with the enthusiastic passion that comes so easily. Some of it is within, but much of it is gaining the energy from other "passioneers." Albert Schweitzer once said, "At times our own light goes out and is rekindled by a spark from another person. Each of us has cause to think with deep gratitude of those who have lighted the flame within us." May this book erupt as a bonfire for you!

CHAPTER 1

Line Dancing from Pregnancy to Labor (First Stage)

Pregnancy to Labor

Families experience bringing forth new life from the moment they find out they are pregnant. Those 40 weeks cause both change and reflection. Traditionally, childbirth educators do not meet expectant couples until around the 30th week, sometimes later. By then, the fetus weighs about 4 pounds, mostly formed and developmentally maturing, and possibly reacting to voices and other sounds.

Reality is setting in that birth is going to happen, and learning about what to expect, and what to do, is what motivates parents to attend class. Many couples have been exposed to well-meaning, non-medical "advice," and may know that the portrayal of media labors is not accurate. It is also rewarding to hear that expectant parents find out that a class is more beneficial than just online advice.

Parents are preparing for the journey from pregnancy to birth. However, often pregnancy seems to be regarded as a separate entity from labor, rather than part of this whole extensive and amazing process. We could speculate why this is so. It could be the tunnel vision of participants coming to class thinking (and sometimes stating), "Just tell me what I need to do," or "If I can just get through this labor, everything will be fine." Or it could be that they realize that pregnancy will end with birth. These beliefs could also originate from providers, who have separate models of care for pregnancy and labor, checking for different health needs and symptoms for each. Childbirth educators can also contribute to these beliefs.

Most individuals realize that our bodies function internally in similar ways, but there can be many, many variables to our systems and body-chemistry reactions. Unfortunately, many educators have presented labor and birth as a "tidy package" based on the commonly used "Labor Chart" showing phases of Stage One, and a diagram of Stage Two contractions. This can be a helpful teaching visual, but it is not as relevant as an introduction to labor. Remember that "relevance" is key to effective adult learning. This, by the way, is why some educators prefer to contain resources within the content/text instead of just a bibliographical list at the end. It becomes more timely and relevant for the reader/learner. Citing in both areas can be effective as well.

Your curriculum needs to include anatomy and physiology of late pregnancy to pre-labor: what contractions are, what they do, and examples of how they might feel before using this chart illustrating average frequency and duration of the phases of Stage One, and diagrams of Stage Two contractions. This becomes relevant to not only tie pregnancy in with labor, but what these lines graphing contractions mean.

Even though some facilities and educators offer Early Pregnancy classes and the previously mentioned continuum, childbirth education is most relevant and effective if it begins with the late-pregnancy part of the continuum as preparation for labor and birth. Unless you are teaching in a clinical setting, as part of a prenatal-care program, the majority of expectant couples have received prenatal care for many weeks, and are quite familiar with nutritional and hydration needs; exercise guidelines for their own situations; body mechanics, discomforts and remedies; and possible warning signs. It is very helpful and supportive, as part of this continuum, to support and validate this information. For some examples, remind them to drink (and possibly eat) during class, be prepared with responses regarding discomfort questions, and remind them, possibly while demonstrating the use of proper body mechanics as they are getting up, as well as changing positions, but not needing to spend much time to get started.

Teaching Anatomy and Physiology of Birth

So how and what do we teach about pregnancy, labor, and birth that will be most relevant and effective? This may be a challenge to meet participants' needs. Tying in Anatomy and Physiology with labor including hormones and contractions can be an excellent start. Even though there has not been a 100% consensus regarding a definite and exact cause of what starts labor, this can begin to give participants an understanding and relatable set of expectations for pre-labor and labor.

The Uterus

Show and briefly discuss comparative anatomy using a book you may give out in class, or charts you may have. This can show what the body knows what to do, primarily caused by hormones, as part of the continuum. You might ask, "If your body knows what to do to form and nourish your baby, won't it know what to do in labor and birth with your help?" It also shows why expectant mothers are uncomfortable. Teach parents about the capabilities of the uterus, and how this muscle organ can stretch to accommodate the baby's growth and create mechanisms to supply the baby's needs. There are 3D uterine models available, or you can inexpensively create your own. Use a 60-watt incandescent light bulb to show the approximate shape and size of a non-pregnant/pre-pregnant uterus, then shop around for a water, liquid detergent or a type of cleaner (empty it out or use it) to demonstrate the approximate shape and size of a uterus at full term. You can also fill the larger container with sand or beans to equal the average weight of the baby, placenta, amniotic fluid, and increased uterus. It is very helpful if you have a permanent place to store this.

The Cervix

From your chart, point out the cervix. Some of your students may not realize that the cervix is part of the uterus when they first come to class. Explain how the cervix needs to get out of the way for the baby to be born. Introduce dilation, effacement, and the purpose of contractions. Educators usually have visuals for these, including charts, or even balloons, to demonstrate. Some educators even have participants suck on a lifesaver to simulate this process. While you are in this vicinity, point out the mucous plug, its purpose, the possibility that they may pass it before labor begins, and its appearance. Also, use your anatomy chart to show the opening of the cervix, which allows the baby to leave the uterus, come down the birth canal, and exit through the vaginal opening. Sometimes, participants confuse the opening of the cervix with the vaginal opening.

Amniotic Sac and Fluid

The baby's fluid is also an opportunity to discuss the approximate amount of fluid, possible times water may break, and how—gush, trickle, spurts—and why each of these may occur. This is also another opportunity to dispel what the media portrays—that everyone's water breaks initially in a big gush. Also, remind participants of the intermittent leaking afterwards as the body is continually still reproducing fluid, and that it should be clear and odorless. Teach them what meconium is, and what it possibly indicates. Although contractions have not been covered yet, you could tell them that labor usually gets stronger after the sac breaks.

Placenta

Teach your students about the purpose, placement, and appearance of the placenta by looking at it (see Third Stage – Chapter 4).

Umbilical Cord

You can use a chart or model. Describe the function, and discuss their partners' option to cut the cord, and how that might feel. ACOG suggests that clamping the cord should be delayed for at least 30 to 60 seconds with full-term babies. Have parents make sure that their providers are aware of their preference. Parents may ask about cord blood donations and/or banking. Be prepared with information and resources.

Round and Broad Ligaments

These ligaments expand during pregnancy due to the baby's growth. They also affect movements during pregnancy, and have a role during labor. It is helpful if you can show the stretching from a chart.

This could be an opportune time for them to carefully and appropriately get up out of their chairs, then lean over, sway, try a lunge, and other movements you may want to include. This not only reinforces body mechanics, comforts, and movement, but introduces some laboring positions.

Lightening

For first-time expectant mothers (primigravidas), their babies will settle or drop into the pelvic inlet, usually between the last 2 to 4 weeks of pregnancy. Use charts that show before and after the baby drops. Then show the easing of pressure on the diaphragm, and possibly on the stomach and intestines. Also, mention that some expectant mothers may not feel much of a difference if they are carrying the baby low in their pregnancies. Then show the effects at the "other end," when the baby descends—increased pressure on the bladder, rectum, pelvic floor, and possibly the sciatic nerve, or nerves of one leg or both. Briefly clarify possible impacts of increased pressure in these areas, being, of course, tactful about the common increased waddling during this time.

In teaching the above material, participants gain more comprehensive understanding of how especially late pregnancy is preparation for labor. It also clarifies many sensations, possible discomforts, and obstetrical terminology.

Pelvis

Moving onto the pelvis can provide a smooth and relevant educational flow. With a pelvis model, you can point out the hip joints, pubic bone, sacrum, and have it adjusted to demonstrate the movability due to the relaxin hormone that is softening the ligaments that hold the bones of the pelvis together. Explain that even though this may cause a variety of discomforts, it allows the pelvis to further open for the baby to descend on his/her way to birth. The baby has to rotate through the pelvis for this to occur.

You may or may not want to use the terms "cardinal movements," "external rotation," and "expulsion." Usually, awareness that the baby's head needs to descend and rotate, and the shoulders need to rotate for him/her to be born suffices.

For a hands-on experience to reinforce this process, I have each couple work together, one holding and opening the pelvis, the other rotating the baby through, then they switch and pass the pelvic and fetal models around until all have had a chance. This technique gives participants a realistic and lasting impression as to what needs to occur. As they are doing this activity, I move on to the significance and meaning of pelvic station, using a chart with the baby in the pelvis, and the lines of pelvic-station measurements superimposed, pointing out the importance of engagement. You may have discovered that some participants are not even aware that their babies need to rotate through the pelvis.

This could be a logical time to begin working on back counter-pressure techniques that partners can offer to expectant moms in order to ease back pressure she may experience from the baby descending, rotating, and possibly during contractions. Have the expectant moms stand up, lean over their chair, a table, all-fours or hands up against the wall. Here, you are further introducing additional labor positions and decision-making skills. At this time, I demonstrate, asking for a volunteer and always getting one, and the partners then try each technique. We practice using thumbs, then fist(s), then the forearm, always going up since it is counter pressure (racquet balls and tools come later – see Chapter 2). I then give the couples a few minutes for expectant mothers to share with their partners what their technique and pressure preferences are. This encourages the communication and teamwork that is so vital to their labor and birth experiences.

Labor

The American College Dictionary states that labor is "bodily toil for the sake of gain." Yes, it is, but it sure can get easier with education, preparation, empowerment, and the many options for comfort. A very significant component is that the female body already knows what to do. The physiological process is there. Even though, as previously mentioned, there may not be full agreement as to what exactly starts labor, we do know the direct involvement of hormones to prepare, continue, and help adjustments afterwards for the mother and baby. Do we need to teach the coordination of all four major hormonal systems that are actively involved in labor and birth: oxytocin, endorphins, prolactin, and catecholamines? Probably not, unless we want to overwhelm our class and witness the "glazed-over-you-just-lost-me" look or "I-just-want-to-know-how-to-get-this-baby-out" look.

Hormones are the reason our bodies know what to do in labor, birth, breastfeeding, and postpartum adjustment and healing. Things that disturb hormones, such as tension, the environment, or medical interventions, may also disturb the course of labor and birth. Oxytocin helps with contractions, birth, placental detachment, and lactation, while endorphins work as natural relaxants and analgesia in labor.

As we discuss the labor process from Stage One to full dilation, we describe what contractions do so couples can understand their productivity and purpose. Show a visual from one picture to the next how the cervix changes during labor. This could be a set of pictures on a chart, in their book, a flip chart, or digital animation—they need to see the progress of dilation and effacement. As previously discussed, the cervix is "getting out of the way." Also, share that contractions help to bring the baby down, making a very powerful combination that is necessary for labor. Help parents understand that contractions help them birth their babies. This will show them that their bodies are doing what they are supposed to do. How empowering!

Class Outline

Give class participants an outline with different categories so they can take notes. We especially focus on Early Labor, since many expectant couples will be at home making their own decisions and need specific information to help them do that. The categories include:

- Contractions
- Possible Signs of Labor
- What to Do
- When to Call
- Assignments
- Practice Plan

Examples of the "contractions" category include:

1. How they feel
2. Frequency
3. Duration
4. Keeping track

For #1 "How they feel," we discuss that it could be an abdominal tightening sensation along with menstrual cramping, and the reasons for both. Perhaps relate this to Braxton Hicks contractions, only now with cramping. Back pressure may be part of the contraction, and that it could feel different for different people. Meanwhile, 2, 3, 4 are components of measuring contractions when they become more regular, and how to keep track using an app may appeal to some couples.

With the above categories, we have discussed relevant components of Early Labor. They have this information to take home to review, they have been engaged in the information, and their confidence is building in having this information. It has also served as a solid foundation for the rest of Stage One. If you would like to see samples of any of the outlines I have created for different classes, please see the Appendix section. Once they have this information and understanding about contractions, now is a relevant time to use the Labor Chart as a more meaningful teaching tool. They can see how the contractions get longer, stronger, and closer together as the body is working harder, and the baby is getting closer to birth. As you go over the different phases, please consider the following to incorporate into your teaching:

- This is only a guideline. Not everyone's contractions are going to follow these exact patterns.
- The timeframes are only averages, and not all labors will fit those numbers.
- Transition does not always represent the "sad face." This can be a very happy and encouraging time; it is the end of dilation and almost the beginning of pushing.
- As you use a Labor Chart to review Stage One, take the opportunity to point out how different Stage Two contractions are because they are doing a very different job that you will be discussing.
- When referring to the Labor Chart, do not just lecture or tell the numbers—what to expect, characteristics, etc. Participants will not remember all of that. Even though you will provide them opportunities for "hands-on" comfort strategies for different types of contractions, give them

either a handout with the information, their own smaller version of a Labor Chart, or point out the information in a class book you may be using.

Notice that hands-on comfort strategy opportunities can be spiraled at relevant times throughout your class or classes, and that only having practice at the end of class may not be as effective. It could be a time, however, to put everything together, but it does not need to be the only time. This can increase retention and relevance of these strategies.

Once spontaneous labor is covered and understood, you can briefly cover Induction here. Consider covering IV fluids, monitoring, pharmacological options, and cesareans during the time of Active Phase. (See Chapters 2 and 3 for rationale if you are teaching a series; the normalcy of labor will have been reinforced first, as well as options for comfort strategies by now.)

CHAPTER 2

Managing Pain

The Power and Wonder of Pain in Labor and Birth

Most human beings fear pain. They associate it with injury and illness. It signals that something is happening to the body that is not supposed to happen, and it needs to be prevented, reduced, or eliminated. As childbirth educators, these beliefs are a challenge we face from the very first class.

Chances are that that is not the very first topic listed on your teaching outline or your curriculum, but parents know it is there. They may have been exposed to misinformation through movies and television shows, and stories from family and friends. They may have had personal, previous experiences with birth pain, and other types of bodily pain.

As educators, we have many opportunities to provide participants with accurate information and strategies to cope with labor effectively. Helping parents understand the nature of pain in labor and birth, with the hormones that underlie this process, can potentially lessen pain if they understand what the body is doing. Understanding that birth is a normal process can empower and build confidence. This knowledge also helps parents speak up for themselves and navigate the many options available. Helping parents internalize these beliefs—that labor and birth pain is positive, powerful, normal, and natural, and a privilege to experience—can be the greatest gift you can give them. This belief encompasses the triad of mind, body, and spirit, and can be quite an undertaking for expectant parents.

Here are some strategies you can use to help your students think differently about the meaning of pain in labor and birth.

- Labor pain is normal and part of the process.
- Labor pain differs from other types of pain and is a positive.
- There are many hormones involved in different parts of labor, including hormones that provide natural pain relief.
- Laboring mothers' bodies will know what to do, just as they have during pregnancy.
- Educators can share the purpose and sensation of contractions, and what they do including frequency, duration, and interval.
- Mothers giving birth are part of a great and ongoing historical event.
- Continuous support is the most important form of comfort during labor. The birth partner can be directly involved, and extremely helpful, in this amazing bonding experience.
- Parent education can reduce the Fear-Tension-Pain cycle and help parents focus instead on Relaxation-Comfort Strategies (see next section).
- Educators can help parents be confident about their upcoming labor and birth experiences by participating in childbirth education classes.
- Educators can tie in the joy factor. Bringing a baby into their families, and the world, is a tremendous reason to celebrate, not a reason to dread pain.

⊚ Participants can understand and internalize that there are numerous comfort strategies that lessen pain, and help parents own and control their experiences.

Teaching parents about the Gate Control Theory of pain can help them understand why comfort strategies work. The goal is to simplify this complex process into ways that participants will understand. The nerve fibers that carry comfort-strategy stimulations to the brain are larger and faster than the ones that carry pain signals. Thus, comfort strategies reach their brains before pain messages because a neurological "gate" can help to block or slow down the pain signals of labor.

A summary chart providing a more extensive explanation of this process, which includes the effects of comfort strategies that use sensory receptors, is in the next section. A Comfort Strategy List is also made available for class distribution to reinforce strategies that have been discussed and practiced.

Pain in labor is unique compared to other types of pain, and has been realized that the standard numeric pain rating scale of 1 to 10 does not accurately assess a laboring patient once they are in the medical setting (Roberts et al., 2010). The variations can be due to individual perceptions and positive approaches, progress of labor, and effectiveness of comfort strategies. Thus, the Joint Commission has now approved a variation of the traditional numeric scale by having the provider ask, "On a scale of 1 to 10, how well are you coping with labor right now?" This demonstrates an insightful effort to help meet the different needs of the obstetrical patients, but not all providers have made themselves aware of this.

The Waltz and Rumba: Non-Pharmacological Pain Relief Strategies

Non-pharmacological pain relief strategies are, of course, at the core of what we teach. We call this a "waltz and rumba" because comfort strategies may be very slow and relaxing, or can be very active. Two significant events in the labor-and-birth world have added a tremendous amount of knowledge and credibility to these strategies. The first is the emphasis on evidence-based practice. The second is the updated American College of Obstetrics and Gynecologists (ACOG) guideline, mentioned in the Preface, regarding the dilation numbers attached to the phases of labor, especially that the Early Phase has been extended to 5 to 6 centimeters.

Even before there was an evidence base, those of us who have taught for a long time knew these comfort strategies worked. Call it passion or common sense, to encourage laboring women to listen to their bodies, and teach them how to enlighten partners in effective ways to offer continuous support. Many obstetrical providers did not hold the same esteem for these strategies, and they considered them neither credible nor helpful. Some even thought we threatened medical decision-making and control. Our attempts to communicate often did not go well. However, a few obstetricians were supportive and open to observing. They admitted that they saw some remarkable differences in the overall experience of couples who attended childbirth-preparation classes, and used what they learned, versus those who either did not take classes or did not use what they learned—especially as the contractions got stronger. In some settings, laboring women can create an environment of confidence, listen to their bodies, and use the strategies they learned. Communication, understanding, and mutual respect have increased greatly between educators and providers, as they regularly see the results.

The 2014 ACOG Guidelines also suggested that low-risk laboring patients stay home longer, with the Early Phase extended. The main purpose of this recommendation, from a medical standpoint, is to "reduce the nation's overall cesarean delivery rate," since many patients arrive at the hospital later in their labors, so there's less reason and time for the "cascade of interventions" to occur. There are, of course, many other benefits. In staying home longer, low-risk patients can be more comfortable in moving about, using comfort strategies as needed, drinking clear liquids, and eating small amounts of easily digested foods, as there is insufficient evidence that proves otherwise in low-risk patients in Early Labor.

Step 1: The Labor Process

Review the labor process: what contractions do and how they might feel. Since low-risk expectant couples will likely stay home in Early Labor, they will need additional information to guide them, such as other possible signs of labor (water breaking; digestive changes, such as indigestion and diarrhea; back discomfort; and spotting), and how to measure contractions when they become more regular (frequency, duration, and interval). There are now a variety of apps available to help parents measure and keep track of contractions, but apps are no substitute for hands-on support.

Describe the big picture of labor: the other two phases (Active and Transition); Second Stage (pushing and birth); Third Stage (the placenta); and Fourth Stage (immediate recovery). Understanding the characteristics during these phases and stages will be most helpful. In the First Stage, contractions will get longer, stronger, and closer together as they efface and dilate the cervix. Visuals, such as charts, the book you use for class, and animated clips, can be very useful and contribute to their understanding. Tactile learning can reinforce this information as well. For instance, if you have a dilation chart, pass it around for participants to touch and feel the progress of the sizes of circles. Also, refer back to their experience of rotating the fetal model through the pelvis and what needed to happen.

With the purpose of pain and how comfort strategies work, parents become aware of pain receptors and gate control, as previously described. To reinforce this understanding, and preface the learning of comfort strategies, we do an activity with the Fear-Tension-Pain cycle. If it is in a book that participants have, they can use that. If not, make them a handout. Have them cross out **fear**, either with a big X or scribbles, whichever they prefer and feels most empowering, and write the word **education** to replace it. Then cross out **tension** and replace with **relaxation.** Next, is **pain,** which cannot be completely crossed out, but have them use a smaller X or scribble to symbolize that pain can be lessened with **comfort strategies** that they also write. So now, we have gone from **Fear-Tension-Pain** to **Education-Relaxation-Comfort Strategies**.

Many participants have expressed how empowering it was to change this cycle from a negative to positive one. This also increases their confidence in the capabilities of mothers' bodies. If class participants fear labor pain and birth, encourage them to ask, "What scares me about the pain in labor?" This can help expectant mothers achieve a more in-depth and accurate under-standing of themselves to possibly lessen the fear and pain, and increase confidence in themselves and their bodies.

Understanding and Responding To Pain in Labor

Mechanoreceptors utilize physical stimuli by transforming this stimulus into electrical energy. This can be transmitted to the brain before pain stimuli.

Julie Jensen, Ph.D., LCCE, FACCE

Receptor Type	Reference	Comfort Strategies
Merkels Disks*	Palms, Soles, Lips, External Genitalia	Squeezing objects, holding hands, massaging palms, standing on a hard surface, "Labor Dance," massaging soles, soles on Jacuzzi jets, sitting on ball or hard surface, lip pressure with Chapstick, kissing or index finger
Meissner's Corpuscles*	Fingertips, Hairless skin	Feeling soft textures, effleurage
Pacinian Corpuscles*	Deep layers in the skin	Cordless vibrator around pelvis or muscles along spine
Joint Receptors	Joint capsules, ligaments, Synovial membranes	Change position, rocking, pelvic rocking on all fours, rhythmic breathing to stimulate rib ligaments

*These are slow to habituate and can be effective for longer lengths of time.

Tactile hair end organs	Hair follicles	Avoid touch going against hair follicles - this may increase pain as these follow same routes as pain

Thermoreceptors respond to heat and cold

Receptor Type	Reference	Comfort Strategies
Thermoreceptors	Skin	Ice chips, cold packs, warm packs, shower, Jacuzzi, bath

Heat		Cold
Increased blood flow and temperature Decreased muscle spasm Increased uterine activity Relaxation of small muscles in skin Elevated pain threshold	Thermoreceptors are usually quick to habituate. Therefore, alternating heat and cold can be most effective. Avoid use on anesthetized tissue.	Decreased blood flow Decreased muscle spasm (longer-lasting than heat) Decreased sensation Useful for back discomfort and joint pain.

Receptor Type	Reference	Comfort Strategy
Olfactory	Nostril – upper part	Familiar calming scents – own items, partner.
Taste	Tongue – taste buds, sour is usually better, produces salivation	Ice chips, popsicles, juice, sucking on textured object
Vision	Eye – retina	Adapt lighting, comforting focal point, color
Auditory	Ears	Music, comforting words, quiet

Adapted from "Elemental Pain Management" Chart, Suzanne M. Alexander, PT Lamaze® International Conference 2003 and "Reducing Pain and Enhancing Progress in Labor: A Guide to Nonpharmacologic Methods for Maternity Caregivers". Penny Simkin, Birth 22 (3)161-171, 1995 and "The Neuromatrix Theory of pain: Selected Nonpharmacologic Methods of Pain Relief for Labor" Trout, K (2004) J Midwifery women's Health, 49, 482-488 (An insight in to the Effects of Personal Perceptions of Pain.) Updated 10/07.

Step 2: The Basics

Continuous support, massage, relaxation, focal point, and patterned breathing are life skills participants are already familiar with. However, they need to learn and practice so they can use them as comfort strategies for labor. These are the basics we will build upon with several other comfort strategies.

Continuous Support

Continuous support is comfort strategy Number One. A person of trust, whom the mother knows well, can physically and emotionally be there to stabilize and reinforce her confidence, remind her to move and hydrate, offer massage and breathing reminders, support her with desired hydrotherapy, advocate for her, bring out the comfort tools, and be prepared to help her with anything else that is needed, as a reassuring presence. It is also helpful to remind the partner/support person to take care of themselves: to hydrate, watch their own positioning and energy, and eat well before going to the hospital. Experiencing labor together can further bond a relationship with the labor and birth process, as well as meeting their baby together.

Massage

Many partners already know a variety of techniques that are helpful and familiar to the laboring woman. Encourage them to use what they already know, and add a few techniques to their "massage tool kit." Work on hands (which have numerous receptors); feet; and counter pressure on the lower back with thumbs, fists, or forearm. Work up for the most effective counter pressure. Also, work on her neck and shoulders, and upper- and mid-back to either side of the spine, working down. Massaging ball joints of the shoulders and hips can be soothing due to the concentration of relaxin in those areas. Massage using the pads of fingers and thumbs can be effective only if the expectant/laboring woman finds this comforting. Massage can ignite many receptors, thus lessening pain, and help with relaxation, as well as the sense of support. The hip squeeze is an example. Some participants like it, and some do not, so I offer two different kinds.

One is a very simple technique, where the partner stands behind the expectant mother who is comfortably and gently leaning over a sturdy table or chair, and he or she rests the heels of their hands on each of the mother's hip joints, and slightly pushes in for some counter pressure, not enough to consider it an actual squeeze, but enough to offer potential relief. The other option is the more standard, but potentially more intense version. Partners stand in the same positions, but use their hands on the crests of the mother's pelvis, squeezing up and in to help open the pelvis and offer counter pressure. This one generally takes individual demonstrations. The knee press is another technique that may need individual, direct demonstrations.

For general massage, switching roles so that partners can be massaged is usually greatly appreciated. It also gives the couple extra opportunities to communicate, and for the expectant mother to demonstrate types of massage she prefers, as well as the degrees of pressure for different techniques.

Massage could also turn into merely touch: holding her hand, putting an arm around her, hugging and swaying together, or whatever the couple works out together. Also, have a variety of massage tools available for the couples to work with to get further ideas for comfort, and possibly purchase on their own. Review the use and benefits of these tools beforehand. Discuss what the partner can do if the laboring mother says, "Don't touch me," how to react, and what that may mean.

Relaxation

For many, this may occur with setting a comfortable environment, with low lighting, continuous support, and massage. Discuss that much of labor involves the muscles. Labor can be much more comfortable, and possibly progress more quickly, with relaxation. Relaxation also conserves energy, and helps the laboring woman's body do what it needs to do more comfortably, and produce the hormones it needs more efficiently. Degrees of relaxation depend on the individual: some relax with movement, breathing, support, and massage, while others want to be in a total meditative state. You may want to include a progressive-relaxation exercise, or walk them through a tense-release activity in your class.

Focal Point

Focal point can help mothers relax and cope more effectively with labor. The focal point can be external, looking at a pleasing item, or internal, visualizing a color, place, animal, person, or whatever expectant mother wishes. Encourage expectant mothers to pack at least one to two items that may become external focal points in the hospital.

Breathing

Since breathing is something our bodies have done for a lifetime, mothers can turn this involuntary process into a conscious one. Slow, even breathing is usually the most effective throughout most of labor. It keeps the laboring woman and baby oxygenated, helps to eliminate the tendency to breath-holding, which can cause tension, reduce oxygenation, and ignite the joint receptors in the rib ligaments. Breathing used to be much more prescriptive. Now it is found that the laboring woman can use it more effectively by finding her own pace. Also, it may be that she finds the use of slow breathing throughout labor to be most helpful, or she may feel the need to alter the pace with the intensity and/ or peaks of the contractions to shallower, more rapid breathing or a slower, deeper pace. Offer the possibilities of these choices and opportunities to try them. Also, encourage the use of deep cleansing breaths at the beginning and end of each contraction for physiological and motivational purposes.

The basics provide a strong introduction and foundation to coping strategies. Offer opportunities to put these together with some practice contractions in a variety of positions for this initial phase of understanding the impact of these comfort strategies, and to build confidence that they will have strong coping tools. When you guide them through simple contractions, make sure expectant mothers are comfortable and stable, and that they have communicated to their partners what they would like for him or her to do (massage, breathe with her, sit with her, hold her hand, etc.). Then time them for a 45-to-60-second contraction, for starters, telling them softly to relax; focus; deep, cleansing breath; slow, even breathing; then, as the contraction ends, another cleansing breath. Have the couples communicate how that worked, and plan for the next contraction. Proceed for as long as the time allows, and however many contractions you feel are appropriate for this initial session, and for your group.

Step 3: Adding More Comfort Strategies to Enhance the Use of Receptors

After we briefly review the role of receptors in lessening the pain in labor, I have already distributed a packet with a "welcome" cover letter, a topic outline for each class, and places to take notes for each class (this is discussed further in the Curriculum Development and Design section). On Class Two's outline, there is a section titled "Receptors," with several lines under it. We review and discuss palms, soles, lips, pelvic floor, movement, changing positions, and conscious breathing. Then they list all five senses. We then review and study the list. I have several props for examples and suggestions to stimulate these receptors for the following:

Palms

Massage squeezing an object (the object could be small or large, soft or hard). I show a dough shaper, wooden roller, melon ball scooper, soft stress-squeezer in different shapes, cut-up buoyancy device (pool noodle), and racquet ball.

Soles

Very easy to stimulate by merely standing, walking, dancing, swaying, standing in the shower, and just resting your feet while sitting on the ball, a chair, couch, or bed. Massage can work as well, if the laboring woman is comfortable having the soles of her feet massaged in labor.

Lips

Kissing, holding your dominant pointer finger above your lips, and applying lip balm.

Pelvic Floor

They know about these muscles from anatomy in Class One. Sitting on a hard, firm surface, such as on the ball, chair, couch, tub (possibly without water), or bed, can relieve pain.

Position Changes/Movement

Changing position ignites the hip-joint receptors, and we already have reviewed and tried several comfort positions that can assist labor progress.

Conscious Breathing

Participants have previously learned about benefits and participated in sample contractions.

Senses

Touch-massage, counter pressure, hugging, slow-dancing, palms, holding hands, squeezing, stimulating soles, tub, shower, and pelvic floor can all relieve pain.

Smell: Familiar scents can be comforting. This can include partner's scent of each other, sentimental items from home, and aromatherapy lotion or oils (maybe just one scent). Have possible samples to try, and give instructions with any oils first.

Sight: Seeing their partner, or other support person, having low lighting, a positive environment, focal points, sentimental items from home, and LED candles, can all be comforting.

Hearing: Encouragement, music (relaxing, energizing, and happy for dancing), humming, moaning, singing, praying, and quietness are all ways for hearing to be used as a comfort strategy.

Taste: Ice chips, small sips of clear liquids, popsicles, washcloth to suck on from home, and lollipops can use taste as a comfort strategy.

Heat/Cold Therapy

The use of hot or cold therapy depends on individual needs. Heat relaxes muscles, and therefore helps lessen back pressure or muscle spasms. In addition, heat increases uterine activity, potentially shortening labor. Cold gives relief to muscles and joints that may be longer-lasting, and helps with inflammation. Both can be pain-relieving and work temporarily as analgesics.

Enhancing Basic Techniques

Some individuals prefer one comfort modality over another, and with others alternating is most effective. Combine many of these methods to stimulate receptors for stronger pain relief. The basics of support, massage, relaxation, focusing, and breathing are then enhanced by adding a few, or many, of the stimulators listed above and below. Some examples:

Measuring Cup

The handle can be squeezed while the cup contains either some aromatherapy or focal point. A set of measuring cups can be squeezed, and then contain a variety of focal points with one cup for aromatherapy.

Sentimental Item from Home

This item could be squeezed, smelled, and looked at for a focal point.

Lip Balm

Lip balm can stimulate and moisten the lips, used as a source of aromatherapy, and squeezed.

LED Candle

An LED candle can be used for relaxed lighting (sight), focal point, and possibly a source of aromatherapy.

Music

A variety of types of music (see above under Hearing) could be used for differences in moods, contractions, and movement. Recently, I saw a framed picture of Bob Marley in a restaurant with one of his quotes below. It read, "One good thing about music, when it hits, you feel no pain." Encouraging for our cause. Wouldn't it be great if it could completely hold true for labor?

Labor Balls

Participants have usually had some exposure to the larger exercise balls, and there are often photographs in the books or handouts that demonstrate properly sitting; leaning over on the floor, couch, or bed; and leaning against a wall with one's back. The smaller-sized ball may be easier for leaning. Many facilities now have the peanut ball that, with its shape, is designed to lean over, lean against the wall horizontally or vertically, or fits nicely between the laboring mother's legs if she is in a side-lying position. This can be very supportive and effective for First-Stage and Second-Stage contractions, as well as during administration of an epidural. Some groups will just take the balls and practice with them in a variety of ways. Other groups need more demonstration and encouragement from you. Most hospitals have these available. Some patients still prefer to bring their own.

These are just to demonstrate a few, but there can be so many possibilities created from simple, easy-to-acquire items that can stimulate the receptors. Think outside the box to combine comfort techniques.

What-to-Pack List

You should provide parents with a what-to-pack list, either in the book you use in class, or as a handout. Reviewing the list can be tied in with the above example list of items. Make sure participants have this out for note-taking as you discuss and demonstrate items that they may want to pack. Suggest that they have the following items on their lists.

Personal Water Bottle

Mothers are more likely to use them if they are familiar.

Focal Points

Familiar, comforting items from home that can be looked at and held, in addition to their phones.

Items to Squeeze

A possible variety of sizes and textures.

A list of comfort strategies that I give out is also included in this section. Also in the packet that I distribute are spaces for recording assignments and goal-setting. Assignments, if you are teaching a series, can include reading, viewing DVDs, and creating opportunities for relaxation; slow, conscious breathing; and massage. They can also include choosing and bringing in their own focal points and massage tools. Encourage research, such as with the Rebozo, and have participants bring in an appropriate shawl for further instruction and practice in using it responsibly. As mentioned in the curriculum section, it is important and validating to follow-up with any assignments in subsequent classes, and provide another opportunity for self-assessment.

The use of accupressure, acupuncture, more extensive use of essential oils, and yoga are all highly recommended comfort methods for pregnancy, labor, and postpartum. However, these are specialty areas. Therefore, I recommend participants research and seek out experts in any of these areas of possible interest.

Comprehensive Situational Preparation Opportunities

I have created and discovered a culminating preparation activity that can achieve the following:

- Relevance to preparation, considerations in a variety of situations

- Reinforcement of coping skills for labor and birth

- Informed decision-making, using previous learning

- Opportunity to put everything together and to better understand the continuum of the whole process

- Educator-observation opportunity to assess self-directed comprehensive learning of levels of preparation

This culminating activity usually takes about an hour, depending on what educator assesses for the group's needs. It is very rewarding to observe the decision-making skills of the couples by now, putting their coping skills together by using some body memory, and the tools and balls. They often create their own laboring positions and massage techniques based on previous learning and class experiences, being mindful of what works for them.

At Home

The mother has been laboring for a while and she decides, or the couple decides together, or the partner suggests that it may be time to begin conscious breathing with the contractions. Visualize exactly where you would be at home, and position yourselves accordingly. Communicate with your partner what you would like for him or her to do during the contraction. A 30- to 60-second contraction begins. Do two to three of these varying the locations at home.

Time to Call

Water breaks, contractions at 5-1-1 or 4-1-1, bleeding, or they just feel it is time. Who does the calling? Know the specifics of how the provider will be reached any time, night or day, and be specific. Your detailed description is all they have to go by. Provider advises that it is time to go to the hospital.

Driving to the Hospital

The car is loaded, has gas, and an old sheet or towel is placed where laboring woman will be sitting. Partners need to consider how they are going to drive safely to the hospital while comforting the mothers. The mother needs to consider how she is going to cope with contractions and stay focused while sitting up with a seatbelt in a moving vehicle. Roleplay the actual driving for about two contractions, and in one of them, the partner hits a pothole, the mother's focus is off, and the partner is concerned about the car's alignment, and trying to comfort the mother.

Arrive at the Hospital

Visualize where to park (become familiar with options from the tour). Park the car. Discuss why it is not a good idea to just drop her off and go park. We have been discussing benefits of walking in labor. Suggest just bringing the labor bag in at this time. The partner helps the mother out of the car.

Walking from Parking Lot to Hospital Entrance

Simulate a contraction along the way. The partner (or the mother) decides to either stop, or continue to walk, and what comfort is needed from the partner.

Arrive at the Entrance

Couples are familiar from the tour if main doors are locked at times, or always open, the possible need to enter through the emergency department, and the availability of wheelchairs, as well as whether they take themselves up to labor and delivery, or if they are escorted. It is also discussed that a contraction may occur in the lobby, elevator, or other possible areas along the way.

Arrival to Labor and Delivery

Pre-registration, and any consultation appointments, were completed beforehand. They are expected, since the provider knows they are coming and has notified the staff. Couples are aware if there is a separate triage area, and what occurs during the triage time from the tour. They then put their blanket, or mat and pillow(s), down to simulate the triage bed. External monitoring has been previously discussed and the purpose of getting a baseline reading. A simulated contraction occurs, including a time where the laboring woman is unhappy about the discomfort of both belts and devices, and being confined, and asks the partner to take them off. Another problem-solving opportunity, since this would not be appropriate for the partner to do.

Admission to Labor and Delivery, and Entering the LDR or LDRP Room

They have seen a room during the tour. I ask them to decide where they would go first, and if they want their partners to lay out all comfort tools and items right away, or to wait. We then do about four to five contractions, each in a different area of the room, changing positions accordingly, using comfort tools. The contractions include strong peaks, and the potential premature urge to push.

Time to Push

We then gather for the Pushing Party (discussed in the Second-Stage section). They can position themselves wherever they can see me, and often they end up in a circle, while sometimes they are a bit more scattered about the room. They can use chairs or the floor to simulate a birthing bed.

This culminating activity usually takes about an hour, depending on what educator assesses for the group's needs. It is very rewarding to observe the decision-making skills of the couples by now, putting their coping skills together by using some body memory, and the tools and balls. They often create their own laboring positions and massage techniques based on previous learning and class experiences, being mindful of what works for them.

Time to Graduate

Some educators distribute their own, or use hospital-provided certificates, especially if it has been a class series. I like to play *Pomp and Circumstance,* and have each couple come up to receive their "diploma," while the rest of the class cheers and applauds. You may also want to give a parting gift, such as a massage tool, depending on your budget. Cutting noodles (the water-buoyancy devices) into about 5-inch sections are very affordable, appreciated, and useful in labor as massage tools, stimulator for palms, soles, and/or for the mother's back to rest against in the tub, or in the car as built-in counter pressure for the lower back.

COMFORT STRATEGY REFERENCE LIST

Continuous Support: emotional, physical, flexible, knowledge of comfort strategies, encouraging, reminders

Knowledge of Labor and Birth Process
Awareness Options
Reframing Pain
Relaxation: down flow
Awareness of benefits: muscles, energy, alert, positive hormone production
Focal Point(s): internal/external

Patterned breathing: deep, cleansing breaths
all slow and even
adapt during peak-faster or slower
preventing urge to push blow

Massage:
- downward (unless using counter pressure for back)
- neck, shoulder, arms
- palms
- upper and mid-back
- counter pressure for lower-back - upward thumbs, hands open or closed
  - one fist/ both fists, using knuckles
  - elbow/forearm, up or oval

- use of massage tool(s)
- racquet ball(s)
- heat/cold

Double hip squeezes
Hydrotherapy
Receptors (physiological processes and evidence-based):
- palms–squeezing items, hand-holding, rolling tool
- soles–walking, standing, dancing/swaying, massage, sitting on ball, chair, couch, or bed
- pelvic floor–sitting on a firm, solid surface such as ball, chair, couch, tub, or bed
- lips–kissing, pointer finger, lip balm

Senses:
Touch: massage, counter pressure, hugging, slow dancing, palms (holding hands, squeezing), soles, tub, shower

Pelvic floor:
Smell: each other, own blanket, pillow and/or stuffed animal, lotion, oil
Sight: partner, other support, lighting, setting environment with accessories, focal points, sentimental items
Hearing: encouragement, music (relaxing, energizing, happy, dance) humming, moaning, singing, praying, quiet
Taste: ice chips, small sips of clear liquid, popsicles, washcloth, lollipops

Position Changes/Movement:
Upright: walking, swaying, dancing, standing, sitting/rocking, bar
Leaning over: chair, couch, bed, partner

Ball: bouncing/swaying
          leaning over
          back against wall
          sitting
All fours
Lunge
Supported squat/squat dangle
Shower/tub
Side-lying

Dancing Examples: All can ignite the hip joint receptors, and utilize pelvic movement and gravity

Slow dancing- Support, rhythm, adding back massage
Waltz- Moderate movement, intermittent opening of the pelvis
Rumba- Pronounced hip movements and a somewhat faster pace
Twist- Shoulder, back, hip, leg and foot movements and usually
       produces laughter

There are many other possibilities or make up your own.

Pharmacological Options and Effects

Just as there are myriad non-pharmacological pain-relief measures that we teach and demonstrate, there are also a few pharmacological options. We help expectant parents understand, through evidence-based information, how and why non-pharmacological comfort strategies work, and those in class should also understand options and effects of pharmacological pain-relief methods, if this is a consideration.

There is the rationale for some educators that if the pros, cons, and the ways the medications are administered are covered, that will suffice and be effective for expectant mothers to make informed decisions. This approach may give some food for thought in that decision, but really is only the appetizer. Informed decision-making is not reached with just pros, cons, and the medical process by which medications are given. Since this is a personal decision, and individuals greatly vary, it should be taken further. Also, what may be a pro or con to one person, may not be the same for another, personally and medically.

What about the decision-making process itself for individuals? The following considerations may take a role in this:

⊙ Having previous pain experiences of their own, or someone they know (even though they know that pain in labor and birth is a normal, natural experience).

⊙ Knowing themselves and their bodies.

⊙ Being aware of their support system and level of

communication.

- Knowing if they are low-risk, and the benefits of staying home longer, and that this is supported by ACOG to potentially lower intervention rates.

- Not considering this potential decision a "pass or fail" component of their birth experiences.

- Knowing how to put pressure from family or friends in perspective.

- Knowing ways of establishing rapport and communication with the labor and delivery nurse regarding their preferences.

Strategies to support the above, and empower individuals in their own informed decision-making process:

- As a responsible educator, be accurately aware of what is available at the facility or facilities where you teach, or where your private clients will be birthing, such as analgesia, light epidurals, or nitrous oxide, and about the staffing: all anesthesiologists, possible ratio of nurse anesthetists, and if there is 24-hour availability, as well as the average rates of epidurals and analgesia.

- An effective introductory question would be to ask the group why a laboring woman might choose an epidural, and the responses cannot just be the word "pain." This can raise their awareness and help with their decision-making. Some possible answers you are seeking would be "exhaustion," "prolonged labor," "blood pressure concerns," "extreme back pressure" (although many back-labor relief techniques have been discussed and tried by now), and "need for cesarean." They may come up with additional reasons, and this can help participants understand more specifics about this decision-making process.

⊚ Ask partners to privately share with expectant partners their thoughts regarding epidurals. This can be very revealing and reinforce the significance of support and communication.

⊚ Briefly discuss how and when an analgesic, or possibly nitrous oxide, might be used, encouraging interactive question/answer techniques to clarify possible benefits, timing, and effects.

⊚ An effective, interactive strategy to cover epidural options is to have a pretty gift box, where the lid can easily come off. Show and explain to the class that on the outside, this represents a very appealing gift that you may want to open, representing the "package deal" of an epidural, with the reality of possibilities that may go with an epidural. These are small, typed, laminated cards. Some sample cards could state:

  ⊚ Usually provides effective pain relief. May feel pressure from the contractions.

  ⊚ Needs continuous IV fluids.

  ⊚ Can lower blood pressure.

  ⊚ Bladder catheterized.

  ⊚ Set up a relaxing environment after the epidural with lighting, aromatherapy, music, and other preferences.

  ⊚ Can get uneven relief; usually can be adjusted.

  ⊚ Causes natural hormone production to slow down, which can affect progress of labor.

  ⊚ May help laboring mom to rest.

  ⊚ Move, hydrate, and empty bladder as much as possible

before epidural is administered.

- This is your decision.
- Include sample of the consent form.
- Continuous monitoring needed.
- May have options: timing of when, lighter dose, or easing up on the dosage before pushing (how this may affect hormone production and increased sensations discussed with this one).
- Communicate your needs to the anesthesia provider.
- Ask questions: be aware of safety to laboring mother and baby.
- Will not be able to freely move about.
- Move legs as much as possible, do ankle circles, and wiggle toes for circulation.
- Can affect ability to push effectively (see laboring down in the Second-Stage section).
- Increases chance of fever and need for treatment.
- Can cause possible itching, nausea, or shivering.
- Could affect skin-to-skin experience and early breastfeeding.
- Could delay ability to get up after the birth.
- Could affect laboring mother's respiration.
- May increase chance of interventional help birthing the baby, such as vacuum extractor, kiwi, forceps (although the rates of these interventions are now low at many facilities).
- May be unnerving to feel partial numbness in the middle torso and upper leg region, or further in each direction.

⊚ May increase chances of a resulting cesarean birth.

This gift package is either passed around the room, or partici-pants pick one out of the box as they return from break. This strategy does not directly differentiate between pros and cons, but can give participants many components to consider. The educator could have each individual read the card they have, and add any further information, or participants could post them with tape after reading. Small group discussions could be used, as well as other techniques. This activity also implies the possible Cascade of Interventions, and could open up more specific discus-sions. This topic could be covered once the class understands labor, possibly while covering the Active Phase, since that may be the timing of pain medication.

Now that non-pharmacological and pharmacological pain-re-lief measures with strategies have been discussed with many examples and experiences, it is important to remember that with all of the differences associated with expression and response to pain, research continues to demonstrate that education and self-evaluation play key roles in the understanding, depth of perception, and overall response to the pain of labor and birth. Confidence and continuous support continue to be reinforced as key factors.

CHAPTER 3

Tango to the Process

Interventions

The amount of time that an educator spends covering interventions, such as IV fluids, monitoring, induction, and cesarean birth, depends on what the group needs, and the facilities involved. Educators should help participants understand indications and risk factors for each of the interventions, and amount of communication that takes place with providers. Basics to cover:

IV Fluids

IV fluids depend on the expectant mother's hydration and possible needs for administering saline, Pitocin, and pain or other medication. Low-risk expectant mothers may not need any IV fluids, or may only need a saline lock (some participants may need that defined). Staying home longer, hydrating, and eating lightly may be a factor in determining this as well.

Monitoring

An external baseline sampling is routine in a hospital setting, then intermittent monitoring for a baby with a low-risk laboring mother who is not induced, and chooses not to have any pain medication.

Induction

Participants should be given reasons for induction, reasons to avoid an induction, and ACOG guidelines regarding this. Couples should be strongly encouraged to discuss with their providers indications, options for methods used, what to expect with contractions and cervical readiness, and the need for continuous monitoring.

Augmentation

As long as a laboring mother and baby are medically fine, the labor process should be allowed to naturally continue. If trying to lessen the time parameters with an amniotomy, or Pitocin is being offered, encourage the couple to be clear as to the reasons.

Cesarean Birth

The majority of participants know what this is, but a short list of indications may be helpful. You should also cover ways to prevent a cesarean birth, that the majority of cesareans are unplanned, and a cesarean birth is not a "failure." Many think that most cesareans are emergencies, probably from portrayals in television programs and movies. Some have heard that the national cesarean rate equals close to one third of total births. Often, you will have primips in your classes, and it becomes important to clarify that that is an overall rate of primips *and* repeat cesarean rates. This can be misleading since the rate for primary cesareans is most often much less, even by more than half at some facilities. Great efforts are being made at many facilities to integrate skin to skin and early breastfeeding into the cesarean-recovery time, if medically possible. This can be helpful and reassuring for participants to know.

In balancing your class time, focus on helping participants understand the normal, healthy birth process, and instill confidence, empowerment, and awareness of their bodies' ability to give birth. Keep the time you spend on interventions proportionate and minimal. You probably have also discussed the importance of flexibility. Chances are that most of participants will encounter IVs and at least minimal monitoring. A minority may experience induction or cesarean birth. Reaching as many of your participants' needs as possible with your original focus, spending long periods of time with 100% of your class for a smaller percentage, will not be making maximum use of class time. I remember the days when some educators would provide many visuals, possibly roleplay, cover many surgical details that possibly took 30 to 45 minutes for that one topic to reach this small number, where in reality, it can be done in a few short minutes. I also remember with a class series, that one night would be the medical-procedure class, and that was usually all that was covered. It does not seem educationally sound and confidence building to expect participants to fully comprehend all of that in one class, and sort out the potential flow of when they may take place. Think about the percentage of class time that was taken to cover possible interventions, primarily with videos and lecture! It just seems so outdated and ineffective now.

For adult learners, it is more useful and relevant to split these topics up into a more chronological and balanced manner, in addition to minimizing the time. As you will see, this is a chronological relevance differing from the condensed multi-purpose relevance technique suggested in Chapter 1. Each one has its appropriate and effective place, depending on the context of the content. For instance, briefly cover induction/augmentation after spontaneous Early Labor, since that may be when most participants enter the hospital (unless there is a scheduled induction or cesarean, which will be that minimal number), and possibly cesarean births after pharmacological pain relief during Active Phase. These are only considerations, but they can flow well, and maximize comprehension and understanding where these potential processes may fit into the labor process for your adult learners. Also, many facilities have found that not many parents attend a separate cesarean class, even when those facilities have a significant percentage of high-risk patients. Part of that reason could be the low rate of scheduled cesareans, or a high percentage are repeat cesareans, so many of these classes have not continued.

Unexpected Outcomes

Some educators describe unexpected outcomes through a variety of discussions and other strategies. Others choose to discuss them specifically. Some of these additional unexpected outcomes include:

- Significant changes occurring in their Birth Plan
- Dealing with unexpected cesarean birth
- The baby needing to go to the nursery for extra medical care
- Precipitous labor and birth
- Parenting concerns
- The baby needing to stay at the hospital longer than the parents
- Fetal loss

"Poop Happens"

Of course, time management is often a concern and challenge, but there is an interactive strategy that can be very effective and lead to helpful discussions. It is called "Poop Happens." I believe that the original idea came from Teri Shilling, who gave me permission to include this, and that may have been her original title for it. I am sure there have been many variations, including the one I am sharing, created since then. I write out 12 potential scenarios on small, sturdy cards,take 12 newborn diapers, colored the inside with yellow and brown markers, and put the cards inside the diapers when the markings were still wet, so the cards would look pretty icky. Then I put these diapers in a small diaper bag and, depending on the class size, either individuals or couples take a diaper. They open the diaper (some have never even held a newborn diaper before), perhaps cringe at the coloring, and read the scenario. They then comment on it, or put it out to the class for discussion. This activity can lead to many helpful insights and consideration of possibilities, and is an effective way to cover many topics in one activity. There is a sample of scenarios called "Possible Scenarios for 'Poop Happens'" in the Appendix.

CHAPTER 4

Belly Dancing from Second Stage to Early Postpartum, and Seeing the Placenta in Between (Second, Third, and Fourth Stages)

Second Stage

Second Stage is a powerful set of forces in this whole journey. How much you need to know, and how much class participants need to know, is your call, but it can be important. Over the years, I have heard childbirth educators express, "How do I teach pushing?" or "Why teach pushing when they really cannot practice it or know what to do before they are actually pushing?" If you take a careful look at those comments, much of that thinking also relates to labor, yet we teach a plethora of comfort strategies for that. Even though some comfort strategies will be used in the Second Stage, it is indeed different because a laboring woman's body is telling her how to expel the baby instead of working to open the cervix. Thus, there will be significant changes in the nature of the contractions, which definitely should be described in classes, as well as shown on a chart or visual in the class book you use.

Just encourage women to listen to their bodies, trust their bodies, and be informed and open to do so in labor, and especially during the Second Stage. Pushing is portrayed as being hard work. It certainly is, but not in the way Hollywood actresses show it with tension, shaking muscles, and dripping sweat.

Patients need to understand that when their providers check them and tell them, "Go ahead and start pushing when you are ready," it means just that. Ten centimeters (or close to it) does not necessarily equal immediate pushing, and certainly if they are not yet experiencing pushing contractions. As they reach the Second Stage, most laboring women will experience two phases to the Second Stage. The first is a Latent Phase, which is an interval. I refer to it as a Rest and Regroup Phase. As the body hormonally regroups, this could be an optimal time for the unmedicated laboring mother to take a short nap, move by walking, swaying, or emptying her bladder, hydrating, or relaxing and taking a few deep breaths. It is also important to acknowledge the partner's role during this time, and remind him or her to get some rest, and to encourage the mother to do any of the above. Also, reinforce that the provider has not necessarily said to push yet, as that is what some partners think they hear and wonder why the mother is sleeping!

The Second Phase is considered active pushing until birth. It is helpful to review from the labor chart or book you have been using as a visual to better understand phases and stages. It may indicate that pushing could be anywhere from 20 or 30 minutes up to two or three hours. That is a significant span of time. Possible contributors to that span are the position of the mother, position of the baby, hormonal activity, medication, and effectiveness of pushing techniques being used.

By now, you have discussed fetal anterior and posterior positions, as well as maternal upright, side-lying, and squatting positions, reinforcing the role of gravity and comfort for the mother and baby. The birthing bed can offer many options and much support: upright positioning, foot of the bed lowered, foot and leg rests, hand grips, and birth bar to allow for a supported squat. Continue to change positions as long as that is comfortable. All fours is sometimes done on a mat on the floor for safety concerns.

Some participants may question whether their babies will fit through their pelvis. It is your call if you take the time to bring up CPD (Cephalopelvic Disproportion). A true diagnosis of this tends to be rare, and is more likely caused by the position of the baby. A very brief response can be given in fairness and accuracy to participants, as well as proportionate time management.

The Second Phase triggers a strong, bearing-down reflex during contractions. Tell birthing women to only push during these contractions and rest in between. There could be several minutes between contractions at this point. In my classes, we have a "Pushing Party" in preparation for these contractions! This is the more detailed version mentioned in the "Comprehensive Situational Preparation Opportunities" section. The partner doubles his or her role as the birthing bed, either sitting in a chair, or beside her where she is sitting on one of two chairs, simulating the birthing bed, or on the floor with a pillow. The expectant woman sits upright, leaning against the pillow, or in one of the chairs, with her pelvis slightly tilted up in a "C" position to follow the baby's direction of descent. I am on the floor or chair with them, demonstrating. They find leverage using their hands, to either grasp their partner's arms or legs, behind their own knees, or rest their hands on their shins, with a good spread to their legs to keep the pelvis open. Before they actually ascertain their leverage, we discuss use of muscles for pushing (see the enclosed Pushing sheet). We also review descent and crowning, and that they may feel that they are working hard at first with no results. We then practice some of the contractions, step-by-step.

Begin with two deep cleansing breaths and, if comfortable, a third breath taking a "gulp of air," slowly bring the chin partially down, but not holding the breath, and it would be more like a "pause for pushing," although they know we are not actually bearing down, just going through the motions. Then I count to about six (as per AWHONN recommendations), and we repeat this about three to four times, so they know that there are usually about that many "pushes" per contraction at this point, concluding with two deep cleansing breaths. Then we do a contraction without any counting, and they pace themselves, so they can get an idea of their preference. This is still the physiologic approach, combined with options and listening to their bodies. We also try an exhale, grunt, or groan rather than a pause for pushing. At this point, I discuss the importance of short spurts for pushing, and the importance, effectiveness, and health benefits of an open glottis.

Here are some other points to discuss during your Pushing Party:

- As birth gets closer, the birthing woman will experience the "fetus ejection reflex" (some providers prefer "spontaneous birth reflex"), where the contractions become even more powerful, and will feel irresistible as a significant release of strong hormones, including adrenaline, take place to help birth her baby. She may want to grasp, and her posture may become more upright and possibly bending slightly forward, and the vulva may open more easily. This can be an instinctual move, especially if she feels well supported and not disturbed or distracted. This is another helpful example of the birthing woman's body knowing what to do.

- "Ring of Fire" is caused by the maximum stretching of the perineal muscles as the baby is close to being born, fully crowning, and to push into it, for progress, and not to be frightened and retreat from it. This is a normal part of birth.

- Beta endorphins naturally increase during Second Stage, if not medicated, and may help as an analgesic.

- The birthing woman may make pushing sounds. These might be deep moaning, groaning, or grunting sounds. This is progress, and partners need to continue with comfort and support, even if they are surprised by those sounds. You might suggest that mothers try one during your "Pushing Party."

- "Birthing down," or "Passive Fetal Descent," could be encouraged if the mother needs rest, or is working with the effects of an epidural. This is when the baby descends without actual pushing.

- There is also the option of trying to time the "wearing off" of an epidural for more effective pushing, but the birthing woman will feel stronger sensations since the beta endorphins have not been naturally released due to the body's reaction from the pain medication in the epidural.

- "Poop happens." Review the proximity of the rectum to the descent of the baby. This bodily function may be part of the birth process, and partners should not be surprised, or let on that this is happening, as the mother may be embarrassed—or mortified.

All this information is shared during the "Pushing Party," greatly increasing the learning, relevance, and retention. Also, continue to connect this with the importance of following what your body is saying, the normalcy of the birth, and how this all can significantly reduce the chances of Second-Stage interventions (episiotomy, kiwi or vacuum extraction, or forceps), and why, with these approaches to pushing, Second-Stage intervention rates have dropped so dramatically.

A brief mention of the "seeding" microbiome as a benefit for the baby coming down the birth canal could be appropriate at this time, where the baby will ingest positive bacteria from the mother. This will help to build the immune and digestive systems. A full discussion of the human flora could be beyond our scope in class, but further research can certainly be encouraged for participants.

This would be an optimal time to discuss benefits of skin to skin, no separation of the mother and baby, immediate breastfeeding, and newborn characteristics. If the expectant mother is still on the floor, or in a chair, it is also a good time to review body mechanics and appropriate, healthy ways to get up.

Who said, "Why or how can I teach pushing?"

Pushing

Pushing can sometimes be as challenging to teach as it is to do!

STRATEGIES TO ASSIST MUSCLE AWARENESS AND DIFFERENTIATION FOR STAGE TWO PUSHING

- Focus on the vaginal opening/pelvic floor area through which the baby will pass; this will encourage the awareness to relax those muscles through the pressure and possible "ring of fire" sensation. Think "down and out," muscles and focus will follow.

- Encourage expectant moms to contract the muscles in the lower abdominal area to push down, as opposed to the facial muscles (purple pushing) or the rectal muscles, since the baby is not passing through either of those areas; make each pushing effort productive in the right direction.

⊚ They can "find" those muscles by coughing and/or doing a deep, cleansing breath into the lower abdominal area; give them a chance to practice this; for further and more specific experience, they can do the "three-finger" pressure hold where they apply three fingers of one hand to the lower abdominal area to feel those muscles contract and push down. Once they master this, some can actually cause the three fingers to rise as they are resting on this area.

⊚ Instruct expectant moms to push into the "ring of fire" and pelvic floor pressure when the time comes and they are actually pushing, not retract from it, to help relieve this sensation and to encourage further descent of the baby.

⊚ To assist expectant moms to be aware of the location through which they are pushing, have them sit upright with their pelvic floor resting on their blanket or mat. Then have them do at least three slow kegel exercises, holding for a few seconds each time; after that, have them GENTLY bear down with their rectal muscles as if they are having a bowel movement. They then can either discuss their sensation awareness as a group or have them reflect individually with their partner on the location difference between these two sets of muscles.

Other ideas for teaching second stage:

_____

_____

_____

_____

_____

Third Stage

Since the detachment and expulsion of the placenta is usually such a brief process, and so should the amount of time be that you cover this stage in class. This topic is a prime example of how much the educator may know compared to how much is covered. While presenting Anatomy and Physiology of Labor (see Chapter 1), educators mention that the placenta is "partly production and partly warehouse" for babies' nutrients and oxygen brought to them via the umbilical cord. Many participants are aware of this, but it is helpful review.

We educators may find it fascinating that the placenta forms so early in pregnancy, evolving from the egg yolk sac. It also is amazing that it becomes an endocrine gland as well, producing the essential pregnancy hormones, primarily, HCG (human chorionic gonado-troph), progesterone, estrogen, HCS (human chorionic somato-mammotropin, also called human placental lactogen or HPL), and helps the ovaries produce relaxin. If this information was covered, your students would glaze over and be absolutely lost, and it would take even more time to bring them back. Some, however, may be aware of some of the hormones due to prenatal tests.

The following points, however, should be discussed as part of the birth process:

- The placenta is usually expelled within 5 to 20 minutes. Some sources say 30 minutes is normal, and others say the sooner, the better.

- The provider may ask the birthing mother to gently bear down. This is to expel the placenta, not detach it, since that has occurred due to the hormones, and the shrinking or involution of the uterus.

- The provider usually asks if the couple (or at least one of them) would like to see the placenta. If you've taught, you know what the usual reaction is to this, even in just class discussion before the birth has taken place. You may, however, want to have a laminated photo of a placenta (small) as an option for participants to see, or possibly two photos, one of the maternal side, and one of the fetal side. Set up a way where this is a complete option, perhaps putting the photo (or photos) in a corner on display for break time instead of passing them around.

⊙ The provider will carefully examine the placenta looking for such things as it being intact, and its size and color. However, brand-new parents are highly distracted by their new baby, who is skin to skin at this point, and may not be aware of this routine process.

⊙ Discuss with the provider ahead of time indications for use of Pitocin, or another type of oxytocin during this process. If this is considered routine, ask why. Encourage expectant parents to share their feelings about this with their providers.

Optional points of discussion, that you can include, but do not necessarily need to:

⊙ Partially retained placenta

⊙ Possible complications at this stage, including implications of the position of the expelled placenta

⊙ Necessities of alternative removal of the placenta

Many educators (including this author) feel that adding the above three points may not be necessary, they are rare complications, and may bring up additional concerns and worry.

Questions may come up regarding options of keeping the placenta for such things as encapsulation, planting, eating, etc. It is important to validate the question, but encourage the individual or couple to do their own research in making that personal decision. Validation is important, as the intent may be culturally based, religion-based, or just plain curiosity. We may not know, and this could be out of our scope of practice. Some participants may be "grossed out" by these considerations because of lack of exposure in our culture, but it still is of upmost importance to acknowledge and validate all questions/concerns. (See the Adult Learner section.)

Early Postpartum

Chances are good that the expectant parents in class are primarily focused on a safe, prepared labor, and are not thinking much about the postpartum period. Early postpartum, sometimes referred to as the Fourth Stage, is a very important part of the whole experience, and should be at least briefly covered. Topics to cover should include:

Skin to Skin

I've found that a significant number of participants are aware of the benefits. It is still a good idea to review the evidence-based information here or, as previously suggested, at the end of the "Pushing Party." It has become a routine experience in most facilities (I have even heard of skin-to-skin experiences taking place in the 1970s). Methods of reviewing can vary, but visuals and hands-on are helpful. Some hospitals have lovely handouts to distribute and review. Asking participants to bring a doll or teddy bear to class, and having the expectant mothers hold them on their chest while reviewing benefits can be reinforcing (even though it would not be actually skin to skin). Share, so that expectant mothers are prepared, that the placenta will be expelled, clean-up on them will be happening, a pad and undies will be put on, and the bed will be put back together, during this skin-to-skin time. Also, explain that chances are they will be working with a nurse, and possibly a lactation consultant, during this time to help initiate breastfeeding. Then have the partner hold the doll or teddy bear while you suggest that they can be involved in skin to skin a bit later, reviewing the hormonal effect from the mother to regulate body temperatures that they will not have, so chances are, their skin-to-skin time will be shorter as things warm up, and the baby should not get too warm. Many partners may not even realize that they can participate in skin to skin during the hospital stay, and certainly at home. Forewarn them, however, about possible nipple confusion, and how and where the baby may be placed.

Cutting the Cord

Many partners choose to do this, but need a heads up before a pair of long surgical scissors are handed to them. Review from the Anatomy and Physiology section that it is their choice. Sharing what it can feel like is reassuring. Review the ACOG Committee Opinion that clamping of the cord should be delayed for at least 30 to 60 seconds for full-term newborns for maximum benefits, and to request that process. The cord will be cut between two clamps that are placed a few inches from the baby.

Lochia

Should be mentioned so that it will not come as such a potential surprise (even shock) to experience that much bleeding at first. More than likely, it is not necessary to explain the whole physiological process of why this occurs, except to remind the expectant mothers of all the periods that they have gotten to miss, the lining of the uterus is now shedding, and that this is a normal, natural, healing process. You may want to show them the "industrial-size" hospital sanitary pad and knit undies, and explain the bleeding phases timetable, as to when they will "graduate" to maxi pads, and eventually mini pads, and how their nurse will regularly check the bleeding during their hospital stay. Share that they will receive further information before leaving the hospital.

Swelling and Soreness

Cold packs are available for swelling and relief of soreness from the birth process.

Depending on the time and scope of your class, this would be a logical time to discuss, and possibly show relevant visuals of routine newborn processes and reasons for the following:

- Apgar scores
- Security devices
- Eye ointment
- Vitamin K shot
- Newborn screening
- Hearing test
- Newborn appearances here or after Second Stage
- Options to consider:
    - Hepatitis B vaccination
    - Circumcision

The benefits and considerations for breastfeeding are spiraled throughout your curriculum, and even more keenly encouraged in your discussion of the immediate skin-to-skin opportunity of that "golden hour." Time may not allow for full coverage of the information, such as colostrum (unless you mention the possibility of leakage during later pregnancy), latch, positioning, diet and hydration, pumping, etc. If you are teaching in a hospital setting, chances are participants will receive much information and help from staff lactation consultants during their stay, as well as after, if needed, and hopefully available. Also, it is likely that breastfeeding classes are offered. Strongly encourage class participants to attend. It may be helpful, however, to give them fair warning about what they will encounter with diaper changes, and what the terms "meconium" (in a different context than the earlier amniotic fluid discussion), and "blow out" mean in this case.

Also, a strong consideration for teaching at this time, and something often not thought of beforehand, is to empower couples to educate family and friends as to what to expect right after the baby is born and during the hospital stay. They may not realize how greatly things have changed, and how different it is compared to the portrayals in the media, or when they were having babies. Make them aware of the following:

- As the mom and baby are experiencing skin to skin for at least the first hour, no one else will be able to hold the baby right way. Also, because of the intimacy time, with possible breastfeeding and exposure, they may not be invited in either during that time.

- Babies are not always weighed and measured right away, so they may not have immediate access to that information.

- Often, all newborn procedures, including bathing (excluding circumcision) are done in the room (possibly the labor and birthing room, postpartum or same room if the LDRP model is used).

- There may or may not be a Level One nursery, but a healthy term baby will experience continuous rooming in with parents.

- Decide your comfort level of having visitors while breast-feeding, and share that.

- Ask family and friends to please not bring large gifts to the hospital. They mean well, but the new parents are the ones having to haul any large gifts home (this is why you may see large floral arrangements left at the nurses' station).

Remind expectant couples to also do the following ahead of time:

- Have the car seat safety-checked ahead of time.

- Choose a pediatric provider ahead of time, and bring their phone number to the hospital to make an appointment, since the baby usually needs to be seen at about 3 to 5 days of age.

- Be clear about their insurance, co-pay, and any deductibles, and that some insurance companies will now cover the cost of a breast pump, but may no longer cover the cost of circumcision, so they are well-informed and do not experience significant financial surprises.

Even though Postpartum Blues and Postpartum Depression may not fall under Early Postpartum, this may be the time to discuss possible reasons, chances, symptoms, and differences of these two possible situations. It would be helpful to either distribute handouts, or refer to a section that may be in a book you distribute in class. Make this a possible interactive activity, at least in question/answer format, or perhaps how to recognize symptoms of possible depression listed on a separate handout. Also, discuss partners' roles in these situations, what can be done, and recognize that partners may also experience the blues or depression. Then, bring the class back to the excitement and joy of becoming parents.

CHAPTER 5

Fundamentals of Teaching: Using All the Dance Steps

"I am not a teacher, but an awakener."

– Robert Frost

Teaching is...

- loving learning;
- giving yourself and your wisdom;
- empowering;
- humbling;
- learning from experience;
- not pretending to have all of the answers and/or solutions;
- having fun;
- letting go of control and not needing the power;
- being open to differing views;
- learning as much (probably more) from your students as they do from you;
- welcoming feedback;
- respecting your students;
- valuing each individual;
- developing your own style;
- encouraging students to develop their own as well;
- opening eyes and hearts, including your own;
- learning much about yourself;
- teaching half of what you know, which is still probably too much;

- learning your limits;
- learning to exceed your limits;
- realizing that...

> *"The truly successful teacher is the one*
> *you will never need again."*
> — Ashleigh Brilliant

- ... and celebrating this.

"I have never let my schooling interfere with my education."
—Mark Twain

Adult Learning and Group Process

> "I am not a teacher, but an
> awakener."
> —Robert Frost

Having a keen insight into characteristics and needs of adult learners is of great value in designing an effective and meaningful curriculum. It also affects your relevant teaching styles, as well as evaluation and feedback. This awareness becomes the basis of the core areas of teaching childbirth education.

It is imperative that a positive learning environment is established. Such a learning environment is essential in establishing successful partnerships between adult learners and educators. The goal should be to develop an atmosphere in which adult learners feel valued, safe, and challenged. Learners are encouraged to become active participants in their learning process with a degree of mutual involvement in determining learner objectives; thus, a needs assessment is indicated at the beginning of the course and at regular intervals. This is further discussed in "Curriculum Design Strategies and Development."

Adults have shared principles that can be useful in arriving at better methods to accommodate their educational needs. These include relevance, motivation, and varied strategies that tap into their experience base. Although educators cannot control whether adults learn, they need to maximize the quality of conditions.

Preface to the Adult Learner's Bill of Rights

Adult education has been one of my greatest passions and blessings in life. Adults have much to say about their education. The Adult Learner's Bill of Rights was created as a relevant, friendly way for adult educators and adult learners to understand their own unique characteristics.

My intention is that adult educators can truly relate to these rights in positive terms. Learners and educators respond more productively to "do's" than "don'ts." This is consistent with the overall approach of an educator to learning. It should be kept positive and encouraging. Each right was carefully written, with consideration of evidence-based research, many years' experience educating adults, and what I feel is courtesy and common sense.

These Adult Learner's Bill of Rights were a significant portion of my PhD dissertation titled, *The Development and Impact of Participatory Behaviors on the Andragogical Learner: A Manual for Adult Educators*. Not only do these Bill of Rights greatly increase awareness and consideration for an adult learning environment, they were created in an alternative format so that the timeless characteristics of adult learners are not just listed or charted, but have the potential of much greater and more interesting impact.

ADULT LEARNING BILL OF RIGHTS
(AS TOLD BY THE ADULT LEARNER)

- Acknowledge my presence.
- Show interest in me as a learner.
- Look at me directly; acknowledge me as an individual within the group of learners.
- I need to know how much you care before I am aware of how much you know.
- Value my experience.
- Respect and praise the fact that I am seeking the information you have to offer.
- Seek my opinions though they may not coincide with yours.
- Hear, see, and feel what I am saying.
- Respect my time.

- Know that I am usually with you by choice.
- Honor my questions with honest answers.
- Value that I am asking questions.
- Be patient with me if I do not get it the first, second, or third time.
- Respect my previous learning.
- Assume not that because I am an adult that basic terms and ideas cannot be used.
- Honor my learning style and plan curriculum with the awareness that there are many styles.
- Provide me with independent problem-solving opportunities.
- Expect me to be self-directed.
- Do not be offended or hold it against me if I do not appear to be participating; I may be learning in a different way.
- Be prepared and organized for me to optimize my learning.
- Be specific with your expectations of me, whether it be in class, an assignment outside of class, and/or materials needed.
- Know that I am responsible for my own learning and participation.
- Seek my input regarding the rationale of the facts and methods that are offered.
- Avoid judgments of my appearance and attitudes.
- Be aware that I have adult responsibilities in my life.
- Have fun, enjoy, and appreciate what you are contributing to my life and yours.

Adult Learner's Bill of Rights Commentary

Since these rights are told by the learner to the adult educator, some strong messages are indicated. This commentary is further clarification directly to the educator. As the conscientious educator, many of the components will overlap in your understanding and efforts.

Acknowledge my Presence

Adults want to be recognized and respected for seeking out the information you have to offer. Give them the credit they deserve in your introductory comments, as well as spiraled throughout the course in a developmentally appropriate (adult) manner.

Show Interest in Me as a Learner and a Person

Adults are coming to you because they have chosen your course. Honor that they are making the time to be with you as a learner, but also as a separate personality.

Look at Me Directly and Acknowledge Me as an Individual Within the Group of Learners

Individual eye contact is a must. It communicates many messages such as that you care, you acknowledge individuals, and that you are confident and enthusiastic, which can be passed on to the individual students as well. Although groups take on their own personalities, never forget that a group or class is comprised of individuals.

I Need to Know How Much You Care Before I Am Aware of How Much You Know

Providing a comfortable and safe environment, both psychologically and physically, is essential to the optimal learning experience. Your body language needs to be at ease, and responses and acknowledgements should be non-judgmental.

Lighting, temperature, noise level, and restroom facilities are important considerations as well. An inviting room arrangement is extremely important. Take into account what kind of communication you desire and arrange accordingly (i.e., semicircle, small groups, or rows with tables and chairs). Make sure participants can see you, and any visuals or displays. All of this will greatly enhance the environment, and strongly portray how much you care, long before learners are ready to receive what you know.

Value my Life Experiences

Adults have a wealth of experiences. Their intent is not to upstage you, but oftentimes they like to share these experiences. It will add substance, and possibly credibility, to the topic being covered, or it may be an opportunity to clarify misinformation. Also, your awareness of previous experiences helps adult learners find the relevance of the topic at hand and how it will fits into their lives.

Respect and Praise the Fact That I Am Seeking the Information That You Have to Offer

Respecting and praising the adult learner contributes to their feelings of safety and comfort in your teaching environment, and helps them turn it into their learning environment. It also enhances your own self-concept that what you are teaching is valuable.

Seek My Opinions Though They May Not Coincide with Yours

When given the opportunity, adults have much to share, and can enhance your class experiences. The confident educator is not fearful of differing opinion, or of losing credibility as the teacher. This can add to the atmosphere of mutual respect.

Hear, See, and Feel What I Am Saying

Actively listen to the adult learner with care, concern, and empathy. Acknowledge your understanding of their questions or comments by using the active-listening skill of repeating the thought back in a respectful, adult tone, while establishing immediate eye contact.

> "Good communication is a balance of speaking and sharing, listening carefully, and absorbing before we speak again."
>
> Anne Wilson Schaef, PhD

Respect my Time

As an educator, your use of the time portrays a strong sense of respect. Begin class on time, as stated in whatever communication was used—a brochure, flyer, catalog, online schedule, or phone call. Do not wait for late arrivals to begin class. This action sends the message that the late class members have more importance than those who arrive on time. Late arrivals are adults. They will figure out how to obtain any missed information and will get the message that you do start on time. End class at the time that is stated and understood. This not only shows respect, but a sensitivity to other obligations that adult learners have in their lives. Giving instructions as students walk out the door is a highly ineffective and inconsiderate teaching technique. Respecting time keeps learners motivated, and maintains an educator's credibility by portraying care and organization.

Know That I Am Usually with You by Choice

The lifelong learner has curiosity and motivation for new ideas and information. Enthusiasm from these students is contagious and can add much to your class environment. Possible resistance and resentment can dissipate as the rights discussed in this segment are respected and followed.

Honor My Questions with Honest Answers

It will enhance your credibility and students' respect as you answer each question directly and honestly. Make sure you understand the question and the concern behind the question. If you know the answer, make it brief and to the point. If you know part of the answer, then give the part you know and do not talk around it. Often, educators incorrectly assume that the more information you give in an answer, the more it appears that you know. Adult learners can see right through this approach and, because of it, may cease to ask questions. If you do not know an answer, simply state that you do not know. If appropriate to the educational situation, you can offer to research the question and have an answer for next time, or lead the student to the source that you feel will reveal the answer.

Try to avoid a common response to a question, "That is a really good question," whether it is to buy some thought-gathering time, or you really do think it is a good question. They should all be considered good questions, and if that comment is only made to a few, that could imply that the rest are not good questions and could affect individual learning and likelihood of asking any more questions.

Value That I Am Asking Questions

If questions are being asked, then you, as the educator, are motivating students to think through the topic presented to the level of internalizing and questioning in order for that information to become part of their repertoire. The safe learning environment (previously discussed) nurtures interactive questioning throughout the class, and helps the educator avoid the awkward asking of, "Are there any questions?" at the end of a topic, only to encounter absolute silence and glazed expressions. Do not forget the importance of reasonable "wait time," however. Be prepared for the possibility of questions being asked out of context at a time where it may not fit in with the current topic. Be tactful and realize that this could just be how this individual is processing, and consider, if you will, answering the question then or at another time.

Be Patient with Me if I Don't Get It the First, Second, or Third Time

Adult educators are often teaching in their field of expertise, and find it easy to forget that many students are, perhaps, being exposed to particular information for the first time. Research shows differing rates of retention that are almost non-existent for the first time. Retention rates certainly increase if the information is presented auditorally, visually, *and* experientially. Be patient; adults want to feel successful in your class and will, with your encouragement and understanding, though it may not be the first, second, or third time.

Respect my Previous Learning

Adult educators have the unique experience of teaching students who have had many previous years of learning and education. Their previous learning usually enhances their experience with you. Occasionally, however, it may be impeded due to previous information, experience, and developed attitudes. Read your students, and be sensitive and respectful to what they are bringing to your class.

Assume Not That Because I Am an Adult That Basic Terms and Ideas Can't be Used

Our words help us understand, empower, build confidence, and make decisions. Use of complex thoughts and vocabulary do not necessarily make a better educator. Many adults develop more respect, and respond more favorably to an educator who can explain concepts in understandable terms. Certainly, correct terminology should be used, but relevance is in the degree of complexity to which it is demonstrated.

Be aware of the positivity of the language you use, as well as terms of reference. Labor and birth are normal, natural, and empowering. Nothing is "incompetent," "dysfunctional," "inadequate," "sectioned," or being "delivered."

Honor my Learning Style and Plan my Curriculum with the Awareness That There are Many Styles

The basic awareness lies, of course, with the auditory learner, visual learner, and kinesthetic learner. Provide related opportunities for all to hear the information, and physically experience the information as it relates to the topic. However, learning styles go beyond these approaches. Many adult learners optimize their learning by asking many questions, re-wording your information into theirs, taking notes, discussing it with peers, and needing much encouragement. Some simply do not. Adult educators need to allow time and activities for all of these styles, as well as have an attitude of patience and understanding. Enjoy and honor your learners!

You may want to complete the "Styles of Learners" activity sheet at the end of this section to gain further insight on reaching varying learning styles and domains.

Vary your instruction and make yourself interesting.

Exclusive lecture has proven to be the least optimal learning experience, yet the most associated with adult learning. Lecture itself can be varied. The adult educator can be standing at a podium, or chatting with students in a semi-circle or, perhaps, sitting on the floor with them. The educator may be using PowerPoint, charts, or handouts as reference points. There are many methods available, even for lecture. Vary these as much as possible. Other techniques include setting up small groups to research and report out, assigning individuals or groups to teach small segments, arranging for a tour of appropriate areas, contacting colleagues, other professionals, or new parents to come in as guest speakers.

In addition to making your class more varied, make yourself interesting as well. An effective instructor needs to remember that no matter how important the information, the mind can only absorb so much. Sharing relevant examples and anecdotes can often help adult learners not only understand facts and figures, but also retain the information presented. Please remember a major characteristic of adult learners is that they can optimally learn when the information is of value to their lives. Keep personal stories relevant and to a minimum.

The use of humor and fun are excellent tools as well. They certainly liven the class and increase motivation for many learners. Even in classes of an intense nature, I have had adults dancing to Tina Turner, doing the Hokey Pokey, and finding new uses for comfort strategies with everyday objects, all with great results. Often, the learners who might be the least likely to participate, have the most fun. Even if you feel that these types of activities may not be your teaching style, expand your horizons and enjoy your teaching as much as your students. Humor is contagious; adult learners do not want their teacher having more fun than they are in class.

Provide Me with Independent Problem-Solving Opportunities

These opportunities could be actively accomplished in a large group, small group, or individually. They can facilitate self-assessments and determine application of information to the adult learner's own life. Problem-solving activities can lead to more effective learning, as well as higher levels of learning. They are also opportunities for feedback and guidance to the learner. Implementation of independent problem-solving opportunities can meet a variety of learning styles, and can be provided during class to minimize the amount of required work outside of class. Think of all the possible opportunities for problem-solving and decision-making within a childbirth education setting.

Expect Me to be Self-Directed

Most adult learners have been responsible for their own learning and behaviors for some time. Do not just hand them answers; facilitate, encourage, give them direction, and expect them to go with it.

Also, count on adults to take care of their own basic needs, whether it's the need to get up, go to the restroom, or move themselves to see more clearly. Also, expect them to ask questions for clarification or assistance, if needed. Another area where self-direction is expected is that of scheduling themselves for regular attendance, as well as completing assignments. You should expect the adult learner to have goals for themselves as to what they expect to gain from your class. This could be in a general class discussion, form to fill out for you, or a goal-setting (needs assessment) opportunity done at the beginning of class, or class series, and revisiting it at the end of the class with a focus on self-assessment.

Do Not be Offended, or Hold It Against Me, if I Do Not Appear to be Participating. I May Be Learning in a Different Way

Educators want participants to enjoy their classes and experience optimal learning. They can even feel frustrated or personally responsible if all learners do not respond with enthusiasm or as expected. It could be that participants have a learning style that is very subdued, or that they are tired, or have something pressing on their minds. Some instructors can even feel a sense of paranoia if a student is not responding how they want them to. Try not to establish this pattern of thoughts, and enjoy your teaching and your students for who they are without assumptions.

Be Prepared and Organized for Me to Optimize my Learning

Preparation and organization for your classes all implies caring for your students. First impressions can make a significant difference. When a student walks into your class for the first time, there is a strong message. If the classroom is set up, displays and materials are ready, and the instructor is available to greet participants, the environment is very positive and caring. Establish procedural expectations immediately, such as picking up handouts and name tags, restroom location, creating their own needed breaks, and their choice of seating. Provide regular, large group breaks as appropriate, clearly stating when class will resume, and follow through with what you state. This is also an optimal networking opportunity. Start and end consistently on time, as previously discussed. Have your teaching materials at hand, and be well-prepared in your subject and in what and how you are going to teach in each session. Of course, be flexible as well, and be prepared for more questions and/or discussion time than anticipated. Always make sure you will have enough handouts, that all equipment is working ahead of time, and music is cued.

Your credibility and earned respect will be optimal under these conditions. If a student requests a copy of a particular article, additional researched information or website, a call or email, it is imperative that you follow through. Take the time after each class to make a "to do" list for yourself, so that you may be well prepared for the next class, whether it be fulfilling requests or specific material that needs to be covered, it will be well worth the effort, and it'll show how much you care.

Be Specific with Your Expectations of Me, Whether it be in Class, an Assignment Outside of Class and/or Materials Needed

Adults want to feel successful in your classes. They want to know what is expected of them as class participants, as well as specific expectations for an outside assignment: the what, how, and when it is due, and how it is assessed; large or small group discussion only, or perhaps, reporting out. It is extremely important that some form of follow-up is done. If the assignment is important enough to be given and expected for the learner to complete outside of class, then it should be acknowledged. It is most deflating for the adult learner to complete an assignment with pride and adherence to expectations only to have the educator forget, or make no mention of it when class reconvenes. Adult learners also want, and need, to know of any suggested comfort tools or materials, the potential cost, and how to locate them. Adult learners thrive on choices (when appropriate) of topic assignments, selection of materials, and systematic approaches. Gathering your students' input to accomplish a needs assessment can, and should, parallel seeking their feedback in assignment determination.

Know That I Am Responsible for my Own Learning and Participation

Adults will learn as much as they choose to learn. Many educators have had to make a significant attitude shift to accept this concept. Often educators feel exclusively responsible for all of the individuals' learning in their class. You cannot learn for a student, but you can certainly follow the above guidelines to facilitate, encourage, and create a positive environment. Once the educator does not accept this full burden of responsibility for students' learning, they can experience more joy of teaching, relate more effectively to their students, and not take it personally if an assignment clearly is not completed, even if the expectation has been clear, as previously mentioned.

As pointed out earlier, a class is comprised of individual learners. Everyone has his or her unique approach to learning, which can reflect in that individual's degree of participation. Again, participation is certainly encouraged by the efforts of the educator, but should not be forced upon any one individual. It is most likely that your quietest students are learning a great deal in your class. Respect the adults' responsibility and choice to learn and participate.

Seek my Input Regarding the Rationale of the Facts and Methods that are Offered

Most adult learners are aware of the reason(s) why they are learning particular information. They are also aware of the various approaches being used. The confident educator gathers relevant information from participants by asking the following questions, and being comfortable with the responses:

- ⊚ Why is this important information for you to know?
- ⊚ What are your needs to set a learning goal for yourself in this class?

- Why are we doing this activity?
- What is the purpose of this assignment?
- Are there benefits from taking notes in this class? What are they?
- What are the purposes of varying your activities?
- What would you like me to know?

I am consistently amazed by the powerful responses to these questions, and the keen understanding that adult learners demonstrate regarding educational value and techniques. Of course, these questions are not asked all at once, but are spiraled throughout content and activities. Knowledge, attitude, and skills become innate priorities.

Avoid Judgments of My Appearance and Attitudes

Perhaps we are conditioned by certain expectations in our society and culture that can cause adult educators to have preconceived notions about appearances of individual adult learners. Educators may make assumptions based on participants' lack of a stylish and well-groomed appearance—perhaps that individual will not or cannot learn as effectively, or they may not have as much to offer the class as others, who are neater in appearance, do. Get beyond appearance and seek the learner. The potential is there for all.

Occasionally, a student may enter your class portraying a disposition of negativity, resistance, and/or resentment. You may think that the best approach is to avoid the person, that it will be easier that way. However, in most cases, establishing eye contact, and using positive-interest techniques, may reveal that this individual is seeking encouragement and acknowledgement, or is simply under some stress. The student may be consciously, or even subconsciously, "testing" your abilities. Get beyond the perceived attitudes and seek the learner; again, the potential is there for all.

Be Aware That I Have Adult Responsibilities in my Life

Many adult learners are at the developmental stage where they likely have full-time jobs, and financial, as well as familial, responsibilities. They expect your class and teaching to be relevant and efficient—time well-spent. While the adult educator should be sensitive to these life situations, it should not prevent the educator from having performance expectations from the adult learner. Not only should activities and content be educationally sound for adults, and time used most wisely, outside assignments need to be reasonable and useful. The adult educator also needs to be clear and developmentally respectful about the results of an assignment not being completed.

Have Fun, Enjoy, and Appreciate What You Are Contributing to My Life and Yours

Your enjoyment and enthusiasm for teaching adults is contagious. A positive attitude encourages intellectual abilities. Students are very intuitive about your motives; examine them regularly. Adult educators often minimize, consciously or unconsciously, the impact they have had on the educational, professional, and personal lives of their students. However, there are a few educators that exaggerate their impact as well. Referring back to the "Teaching Is..." document, please do not lose sight of the fact that teaching is empowering, yet humbling. Let go of the control. You do not need the power. Learn your limits, and learn to exceed your limits. A sequential, compartmentalized approach is limiting and unrealistic. Allow yourself and your students creative flexibility within the expected guidelines. That may seem contradictory, but can be achieved through awareness and balance.

Respecting and applying the "Bill of Rights" to adult programs and teaching will create a powerful partnership between educator and learner. Adults have a need for immediacy of application of information. They engage in learning largely in response to pressures they feel from current life situations. Education becomes a process of improving their abilities to deal with life's concerns that they are facing. Adult learners generally are problem-centered, so the adult educator needs to focus on being person-centered. Adult learners are what they have done. Adult educators are what they can teach. Teachers are the facilitators, guides, resources, and process managers. They release the energy of others; it is in the approach, not just the content.

Curiosity and desire are key considerations, as well. Adults take responsibility for their own learning through self-directed inquiry. They also can usually learn collaboratively with the help of other participants and a supportive educator who can also facilitate understanding and respect of commonalities and diversities.

Motivation drives adult learners to attach to their own learning. It prompts the dyadic (two-part) process for the adult educator to facilitate the adult learner to discover. Opportunities are offered by the factors of the environmental and educational situation. Adults will learn what they choose to learn through motivation and the sense that their needs are being met from the original needs assessment, as well as, possibly, seeking further information through questions and discussions.

Adults also need to test the instructor's ideas against their own. One of the critical motivators for adult learners is their assessment of the discrepancy between their current knowledge base and where they want or need to be. The adult educator

should provide the learner with the tools (and possibly procedures) for obtaining data and making responsible judgments
about their developmental level of competency. This, of course,
requires the provision of a safe, supportive and, non-threatening
atmosphere for what could be a very humbling experience for
many adults. Be aware of, and facilitate, their active participation
in the process, goals, and evaluation of their own successful
learning. Listen to adult learners. They have much to say about
their own learning. Adult learners often, and sometimes unexpectedly, teach adult educators about life, themselves, and a
variety of subject areas. Embrace and treasure those times for
yourself and your learners.

There are many factors that will add up to success for adult
learners, and an understanding and acceptance of oneself as a
learner. In adults, learning will take place, for the most part, only if
learners take the initiative, and are allowed to diagnose their individual needs. The adult learner needs relevant experiences, and to
be able to contribute to the development of a conducive learning
environment. Adults will not successfully learn under conditions
incompatible with their self-concept. Because andragogy recog-
nizes this understanding, these characteristics become a relevant
and meaningful tool to reach adults.

When adults perceive their learning destiny to reside within
themselves, they are free to be creative and productive. The more
they feel their unique potential is being used, the greater their
achievement will be. The adult educator is responsible for offering
adult learner challenging opportunities and delegating the responsibility back to them. Cooperation and learning are an interesting
pair of terms. Cooperating with one's learning can open myriad
horizons, especially with the adult learner who can possess the
full consciousness of this process. Giving learning a fair chance,
and welcoming the idea of lifelong learning, can maximize the

openness to new information, skills, and experiences for both the adult learner and the adult educator.

This has been an organized effort to extend my knowledge and understanding of adult learning behaviors to the receptive and willing vessels, as well as fellow passionate adult educators. Experience and understanding can give us assurance. William Arthur Ward once said, "The mediocre teacher tells. The good teacher explains. The superior teacher demonstrates. The great teacher inspires." I sincerely hope we all aspire to be that great teacher.

STYLES OF LEARNERS

LEARNING DOMAINS

These are the actions or thoughts applied to the approach of learning:

- Cognitive– understanding and application of ideas
- Affective– finding the relevant value with interest
- Psychomotor– action-oriented habitual learned response with some confidence and skill

LEARNING STYLES

- Auditory– listening, discussing, reading aloud
- Visual– taking notes, looking at instructions and illustrations, finding handouts helpful
- Kinesthetic– responding and learning with movement, having sense of balance and rhythm

How does your style of learning affect your teaching?

_____

_____

_____

Name some specific characteristics that you can observe that will help you determine the learning styles of your participants.

_____

_____

_____

_____

Check off what Domains and Styles each of these activities meet:

ACTIVITY	LEARNING DOMAINS			LEARNING STYLES		
	Cognitive	Affective	Psychomotor	Auditory	Visual	Kinesthetic
Introductions						
Floor practice-relaxation						
Lecture on Anatomy and Physiology						
Discussion on Birth Process using visuals						
Homework Research on Epidurals						
Role-play Labor Scenarios						
Hospital tour						
Labor stations						

Childbirth Education for Expectant Adolescent Parents

It takes special interest, heart, and patience to be an effective childbirth educator for expectant teen parents. Many of the Adult Learning Bill of Rights previously discussed apply to teaching teens, especially the ones regarding acknowledgement, value, and listening. Avoiding judgment in appearances and participation are essential. If you can have fun and enjoy them in class, this will go a long way with teens. Your interest and care go even further. The following are a continuation of the Bill of Rights, especially geared for teens:

- Respect me as an expectant parent.
- Actively listen, and that will help me to build trust in the class environment that you are providing.
- Use appropriate humor as you vary your instruction to meet my unique needs.
- Be kind, accepting, interested, and interesting.
- Respect that I may be overwhelmed and scared, but I did come to your class seeking information.
- Use correct vocabulary and do not talk down to me, even though I am young.
- Encourage me to make my own decisions.
- Understand that I may, or may not, participate in the discussions, activities, and the practice of comfort techniques.
- I am responsible for my own learning, but help me.
- Respect and honor if the teen father attends class.
- Value additional support that I may have, and be empathetic to any circumstances or family dynamics that could present themselves.

- Give me the reality of parenting, but do not lecture or judge, especially in a way that I could interpret as being non-supportive.

- Encourage me to complete my schooling and plan for my future.

Educating teens in a childbirth education setting can feel endearing, perplexing, challenging, and, possibly, intimidating. Once they gain your trust, and are comfortable and accepted in the environment you provide, they may share stories and or circumstances that could cause you to feel uncomfortable at times. Below are possible examples for which to be prepared:

- The circumstances of their pregnancies and their home environments may be difficult.

- They may lack support from the baby's father.

- Their families may not accept the situation or the baby's father.

- They do not want their babies or to experience labor.

- They may have unrealistic expectations of parental responsibilities.

- They may have a relinquishment arrangement and information about the adoptive parents.

- They are no longer allowed to live at home, and cannot financially support themselves and a baby.

- They do not want to rely on their parents, but have to.

- They expect parents to do much of the care so they can go to school, work, or resume their teen life.

Their self-worth and identity could be greatly impacted. They may feel confused as they have one foot in the adult world, and the other in the teen world. Nutrition and regular prenatal care are of extreme importance, as well as the benefits of breastfeeding, and generally more time is spent on these topics in a teen class. They may be in a program for teens that can provide extra support. Find out, as it is helpful for you to know.

I had the privilege of teaching in two different teen programs. One was through a hospital where the teens had a great deal of support, and were offered incentives, earning points for attending class, going to prenatal care appointments, and staying in school. With points earned, they could "purchase" baby items. Another was through a high school, where they had their own area and daycare, so they had childcare as they returned to school. Both of these situations offered nutritional snacks and drinks during the class, as well as gift packs for the end of class, which was a big incentive for teens. State, county, and a variety of business funding helped support these programs.

Encouraging involvement and participation may take special effort and considerations. Opportunities for peer discussions in the large group, or small break out groups, can be helpful. Recruiting guest speakers can be most effective, especially a teen mother, or couple with their baby who were in one of your previous classes. They can answer questions and discuss what helped them in labor and birth, and the impact on their lives now.

I was the mother of an adolescent mom who was also willing to come in with her son to share her experiences with the family support, friends, and schooling. She was a great inspiration as she went on to finish college, and graduate with honors, with the responsibility of a child. She came in several times at different stages of these accomplishments.

Teaching and practicing comfort strategies will take keen insight. Survey the group to gauge participants' comfort levels, especially with the relaxation and massage portions of your class.

You may need to shorten this session, but still include the basic teachings and the benefits. Also, it can be helpful if you create a simple form for them to fill out with their labor and birth goals, and another with questions for their providers, once you have clarified options they will have. Give them an opportunity in class to complete these with their support person or family members. Also ask them to include educational goals and needs for support. Ask for volunteers to share as peer encouragement, if you feel it would be appropriate for the group you have.

You may also want to provide a nicely formatted form for the expectant teens to write a letter to their babies. Depending on your population, writing skills may greatly vary. You can give them the option of drawing a picture instead. This can be done later, on their own, or as part of a class. This provides another opportunity for sharing.

If you have access to video clips, especially for expectant teens, these can be useful to show and introduce them to the realities of contractions, immediate newborn appearance, skin to skin, Third Stage, lochia, and body shape. They may have no idea or sense of what to expect right after birth. Validate and value their questions and concerns, no matter how basic or out of context they may be, or how gross they may feel these realities are. A question box may be an alternative if the group hesitates to openly ask questions or express concerns. That has rarely been needed, however, with the teen classes I have taught. Also, discuss how they are going to handle visitors in the hospital and home. Often, they may have large groups of friends who want to see the baby, and this may be a challenge to manage with baby care, breastfeeding, and them now being different than most of their friends.

If time allows, have them share concerns regarding their

pets. Many teens have a strong attachment to a special pet, or pets, and are not sure how to balance that with a new baby. As you discuss what to pack, suggest a picture(s) of their pet(s) (chances are, they have several on their phone). Also, many adolescents have attachments to a stuffed animal or blanket. Encourage them to pack either or both of these to have with them at the hospital.

Teens and phones: a synonymous pairing, as we know. Simply ask that they be courteous with their phones. Take it a bit further if you feel you need to set more boundaries, such as no phones out or texting in class. You do not want distractions from their learning, nor a potential power struggle with the phone usage. Find a compromise. An activity with them using their phone, such as looking something up, finding a focal point, or possibly sharing a few seconds of possible music they may use in labor could work as possibilities.

Another consideration is that often many of the expectant adolescents' mothers (and sometimes, fathers) are with them in class. Find ways to validate their presence, as well as suggestions regarding labor and postpartum support. They often sought out my input and suggestions, knowing that I also was the parent of an adolescent mother. Sometimes we were able to have a small group discussion as the teens were working on one of their goal sheets or their letters to their babies. As mentioned earlier, there may be some challenging family dynamics, or it could be that these parents just want to support and help their teens.

Up to this point, this section has focused on the teen childbirth classes. That, however, is not always the case. So much depends on the offerings and resources available. I am always in such awe of the courage that a teen must have to attend a more traditional class of primarily adults. Educators offering a welcoming validation will help adolescent participant(s), and provide a positive model and cue to the adult participants. Teen participants can also make the balancing act childbirth educators consistently face more precarious. However, accepting them, and not focusing on their presence as someone "different," is key. Appreciating them will help integrate their needs within that of the group, keeping in mind the first four statements of the Bill of Rights:

- Acknowledge my presence.
- Show interest in me as a learner and as a person.
- Look at me directly. Acknowledge me as an individual within the group of learners.
- I need to know how much you care before I am aware of how much you know.

If you are teaching, or considering teaching, an adolescent childbirth education class, enjoy them and have fun with them. Ask them if certain activities would be helpful or appropriate, and they will usually tell you. I worked with expectant teens for many years. I have fun with them, and have witnessed the support that many of them had. For those who did not, as a mother and "caretaker of the world," I wanted to just bring some of them home with me. Your heart cannot break for them, but it has to work with them.

It takes a special heart, but with an attitude of objectivity to be with them, teach and respect them, you can make a difference in preparing them for their new lives. Often, their courage and determination can enter that open heart of yours and inspire you! What a privilege it is to share that preparation with adolescents. One of the most memorable and meaningful comments I ever received on a class evaluation was from a 16-year-old expectant father (who definitely had to be a social challenge in many ways, though not in my class). He wrote, in big letters: "JULIE ROCKS! SHE REALLY CARES ABOUT US!" Enough said.

Curriculum Design and Development

Curriculum: a powerful concept and word, and even more, an absolute necessity with many components. Your curriculum is you. Attempting to teach without a strong curriculum would be about as effective and efficient as a surgeon operating on a patient knowing nothing about their physical condition, or participating on the Olympic Swim Team when you can barely doggy paddle, or driving a semi-truck across the country when you do not know what a clutch is. Obviously, these illustrations could go on and on.

The affective component is that you feel proud and positive about your curriculum. These feelings will reflect in your teaching. Even if it is a facility-standardized curriculum, you still add part of yourself. Chances are, a standardized curriculum may only be an outline of topics that you should teach in each class, but does not include strategies, times, activities, and the "you" that you bring to it.

In designing, redesigning, or tweaking a curriculum, relevance is the absolute key with adult learners. The following are essentials:

- Evidence-based information and reinforcing its relevance
- Flow of information and activities
- Appropriate amount of information
- Realistic times/breaks
- Proportionate time spent on topics
- Spiral the information and activities
- Overall goals for your class or series
- Objectives for specific topics, with areas and methods for evaluation of these objectives
- Varied and effective adult-learner teaching strategies

- Appropriate and limited handouts

- Acknowledgment of each handout

- Review/preview during opening and closing of each pertinent class

- Opportunities for questions and discussions

- Note-taking opportunities

- Participant preparation for the flow of normal labor from pre-labor through the Fourth Stage

- Informed decision-making facilitation by providing empowering information of options

- Identification of the positive role of pain during labor and birth, and the importance of continuous support

- Promotion of non-pharmacological pain management strategies to encourage confidence and incorporate knowledge of expectations

- Provision of information that empowers while creating chances for spiraling, and ample time for hands-on reinforcement of comfort strategies to build on previous learning

- Presentation of information about medical interventions: indications, options, and effects. Do not clump all medical interventions in one chunk of a class. Help participants learn more effectively by discussing this information in a less overwhelming, and more chronological way. This can use spiraling, as well as learner needs and retention. For example, consider the rationale (or lack of) in covering fetal monitoring, induction, pain medication, Second-Stage interventions, and cesarean birth altogether in one class. It becomes ineffective, overwhelming, and can impact the positivity of their learning.

Implementing your curriculum effectively will include balancing more challenging than any circus act since you will need to be aware of and do the following:

- Create a comfortable, safe learning environment where participants can become empowered with awareness of the labor and birth process, know their options, and take ownership of their labor and birth experiences. This could also make you a magician, since many participants may enter your class knowing only that this baby is going to come out, and that may be about it, along with participants who have a medical background. Or you could have the person who repeats all the horror stories they have heard. Or the individuals who have acquired a lot of misinformation. Remember, create a comfortable learning environment.

- Stay on track with the information and flow, even with possible off-track questions, by varying your strategies.

- Carefully observe your group.

- Carefully observe your individuals.

- Transition smoothly from topic to topic.

- Keep close track of time, and stick to starting and ending times.

Did I say magician? Perhaps miracle worker may be more accurate. The above could also be considered overall goals.

How can we be the caretakers of the world, and teach objectively something we are so passionate about, without feeling conflicted? This can occur whether you are teaching in a hospital or a private setting. Remember, your approach and attitude carry over to your participants' birth experiences. Even if they are educated, professional adults, they may choose options you feel are right. Stay passionate, but supportive. Remember, you are now the "miracle worker." You have such a limited time to prepare participants for the most significant, spiritual, and connecting journey of their lives.

You may want to consider putting your thoughts together and write out your birth philosophy. If, where, and with whom, you share this would be completely up to you. I have chosen to share mine with you.

My Birth Philosophy

Birth. How do I explain a full being miraculously emerging from a tiny, tiny egg in a matter of 40 weeks? I'm so in awe of this process that I want to shout for joy. So, I cannot just tell it, but I feel it and channel this passion into guiding emergent parents to fully engage in the birth of their creation.

I humbly lead each woman in her quest to realize that, "Yes, I can do this. My body does already know what to do! My partner can be my co-star in this miraculous production of becoming a new family!" Witnessing their eyes light up is magical. How this natural process can so profoundly impact and access our hearts, souls, and inner wisdom—personally and professionally—is, indeed, a true spiritual experience.

We now have access to an abundance of evidence-based information we can share with expectant parents, building their confidence to make choices that are true to themselves, and that bridge the gap between a natural journey and the medical world. Oh, yes, I am truly blessed when I can help guide and contribute to the miraculous world of birth as a woman, mother, grandmother, educator, mentor, coordinator, and, thankfully, so much more.

Content, Format, and Materials

The initial format of your curriculum design may need to follow the requirements of the program you attend as part of your certification. However, since this is what you will be teaching from this, make it as relevant and useful for yourself as you can. Will it be formatted in columns for content, time, objectives, and strategies? Will it be in outline form? Page numbers can certainly be helpful, too. How detailed will it be? Can it directly be used for your teaching notes?

You will need a list of materials for each class. This also provides you with quick reminders while setting up your classes. You may be given a list of required topics. These can then be adapted to your own teaching situation. A short list of broad-based goals will allow you to put your passions for teaching childbirth education into a class format. These may also tie in with your Birth Philosophy. Asking yourself "Why am I teaching this?" can give you some direction as well. A few examples of teaching goals are as follows:

- Participants will understand and appreciate that labor is a normal, natural process.

- Expectant parents will gain confidence through demonstrating and applying numerous comfort strategies.

Constructing at least one measurable learner objective, using an action verb for each major topic, may also be required by your program, and is certainly an educationally sound way to keep your instruction purposeful and focused on your participants' learning. For example:

- By the end of Class One, students will be able to describe at least three possible signs of Early Labor.

- By the end of this class series, participants will be able to identify how each of the five senses can be used to help minimize labor pain.

⊙ By the end of Class Two, participants will be able to list at least three benefits to continuous support in labor.

Please see the following list of suggested measurable terms that could be appropriately used in constructing your objectives.

EXAMPLES OF APPROPRIATE ACTION VERBS

OR MEASURABLE TERMS THAT COULD BE USED TO CONSTRUCT MEASURABLE OBJECTIVES

- ⊙ Recognize
- ⊙ Compare
- ⊙ Identify
- ⊙ Describe
- ⊙ Demonstrate
- ⊙ Discuss
- ⊙ Contrast
- ⊙ Develop
- ⊙ Construct
- ⊙ State
- ⊙ List
- ⊙ Define
- ⊙ Summarize
- ⊙ Give Examples of
- ⊙ Explain

Each objective should have a teaching strategy or method to accurately determine the accomplishment of the objective and the impact on participants' learning. How do you know they are "getting it?" Create opportunities to simply ask at times, "How is this relevant for you?" or "How can you use this in labor or birth?" as previously discussed.

Use breaks as teaching strategies as well. Encourage participants to network by suggesting they talk to other participants, possibly giving them specific questions to ask. Most couples will do a good job of returning on time, especially if you give them a specific time. Consider making the return time an odd number, such as 7:07, and make sure your room clock is accurate for their return. Also, dangle a "carrot" for their return, like "As soon as we get back, expectant moms are going to get a back massage," or "We will be starting the video segment." Be consistent and resume class at the time you say. This is a positive message and motivation of consistency for their prompt return, and keeps things on track. Of course, breaks will be regular, and encourage participants to take their own breaks when needed. Also encourage them to eat and drink freely in class. Even though there will be a significant amount of movement in class, there are times when you need to be mindful that "The mind can only absorb what the seat can endure."

These strategies are designed to help educators support learners in establishing ownership of their learning. This will be an individual journey of personal investment in one's preparation for such a life-altering experience, of discovering how this will fit into their own experiences, and setting their expectations and goals. Vary your strategies to enhance the participants' learning and peak interest. Please see the provided list of ideas to reinforce the variety. These tips are also an example of spiraling some key points, as taken from the Adult Learning section.

TEACHING STRATEGIES

- Lecture: interactive, involving the group, such as feedback and asking them to finish your sentences.
- Needs Assessment
- Icebreakers
- Break-out Groups
- Handouts
- Models/Props
- Demonstration/Return Demonstration
- Interactive Discussion
- Question-Answer
- Video Clips
- Power Point
- Homework Assignments
- Scenario Cards
- Stories/Sharing
- Bags with Visuals (for points of presentation and discussion)
- Introductions– or other methods of sharing
- Setting the Environment: Music, Lighting, Arrangement, Displays
- Validation (of concerns, questions, choices, beliefs)
- Wait Time
- Research (educator and/or participants)
- Tours
- Situational Practices
- Modeling
- Spiraling

Determine your time goals for each topic or activity so that your time management is effective, and that you are keeping topics in proportion and prioritizing them. This may also be tied to your goals and objectives. Please allow for breaks, questions and discussions, and review and preview for the next class. Expectant mothers also need time to move as you transition to a variety of activities. Allow additional time for couples to have some individual processing time to enhance communication, especially regarding preferences for comfort strategies.

Getting Started Techniques

Nametags

This may sound like such a minor housekeeping detail, but it can speak volumes to your participants. Create an opportunity to either obtain your class roster prior to the first class, or allow extra time before your first class, so you can make nametags ahead of time. Nametags can be simple stick-ons, pin-ons, or lanyards. Some educators are creative with shapes of nametags, such as a baby, diaper, or a ten-centimeter circle. Whatever is used, if the nametags are prepared in advance, participants feel welcomed and expected, instead of entering the class and writing out their own. Another advantage is that if you write them out, you have a chance to write each name largely and clearly, and you will be able to read them! Handwritten nametags also feel more welcoming than computer-generated ones.

Introductions

There are many ways to approach these in effective and timely ways. You can get so many ideas by networking with other educators. Childbirth educators are the most generous, sharing group I know. I do not have participants do this at the very beginning in order to give them time to acclimate to their environment, and after announcements and review of handouts. Also, I do not refer to them as "introductions," but as "sharing." It seems to ease the idea of speaking to a group for those who have that concern. I have them share their first name, due date, baby's sex (if they would like), and their motivations for being in class. This also ties in needs assessments for you and the group, and allows them to see how much they have in common. Determine if you or the class really need to know their occupation, or other personal information, depending on the population (demographics) you generally have in your area and classes.

Chances are, you may choose to introduce yourself at the beginning. How much do you share about yourself to establish credibility and interest, as well as stay within your comfort level? Make it brief, relevant, and not overly personal, although interjecting very short, appropriate, personal experiences can be effective at times in your class(es), and examples and anecdotes to bridge concepts and ideas for them. Most seem to enjoy these.

There are such a variety of strategies that can be used to assess the needs of your class. In addition to the above-mentioned sharing opportunities, such as:

- Having participants write their needs on posted chart paper, and cross them off as they are met.

- Come up with a list in break-out groups, either by splitting the class in couples, or by gender, then share with the group.

- Have an "idea" or "needs" box that they can write ideas and put them in the box, and a volunteer, or the educator, can read them at relevant times. Discussion can follow.

⊚ Another pre-and-post activity could be an individual handout where each participant writes down initial needs, then by the end of the class, or class series, could self-assess, then possibly share so that the large group can benefit from any information volunteers are willing to share.

⊚ Simply ask a basic question (reminding them about this being a safe environment to express themselves), such as, "How many of you know that this baby has to come out, but little else about labor and birth?" I continue to be amazed on how many will indicate "yes," and how willing they are to show their vulnerabilities and need to learn more.

There are brief, effective ways of dealing with those who choose to share "horror stories" they have heard. I usually just smile and say, "consider the source." Also, a way to bring up the exposure of misinformation is to point out the Hollywood births, and what they repeatedly see for labor and birth, and how this experience is highly misrepresented. In contrast, remind them that the class content is accurate and evidence-based.

Handouts

If you use an effective and complete commercial book, your handouts can be minimal. Make sure they are appealing, legible, relevant, brief, attractive, and not direct repeats of what is included in the book you may use. As previously mentioned, I also provide a packet that includes a Welcome Cover Letter, and an outline of topics covered in each class. These outlines also provide note-taking opportunities, and places for assignments and practice goals. If it is a series, we self-assess these goals the following week, which can be very motivating. These are available to you upon request, as previously offered (more spiraling).

Acknowledge and review each distributed handout. If it is important enough to give out, it is worth reviewing. That is a strong message. Create documents that are friendly and invite learners to read them, and that encourage relevancy and further learning. The information you distribute should balance between brief and review reinforcement, and supplementary information. Make sure the handouts are not taking the place of instruction, and that any listed resources/websites are current. Provide folders to keep their materials together and organized. Be aware of the use of empowering language and positive terms in your handouts, as well as your general teaching. (More specifics were mentioned in the Adult Learning section.)

Spiraling

Since we are continuously aware of maximizing our information in the best use of our time, spiraling our curriculum is a highly suggested technique. The most effective adult learning is in small doses and building on previous learning. Spiraling is a great way to reinforce the natural birth process, build confidence, help solidify the effectiveness and use of comfort strategies, and clarify benefits of breastfeeding. You can refer back to a video clip that you've shown. If you are in a hospital setting, and your class includes a tour, take the tour before a situational practice, so that participants can connect the use of comfort strategies with the hospital setting they have already seen, perhaps at the beginning or middle of a class. Remember, the key with adult learners is RELEVANCE. A tour at the very end would not effectively reinforce decision-making and use of comfort strategies nor, be as relevant to visualize the use of comfort strategies as discussed and practiced in class.

Using Power Point in a Childbirth Education Classroom

We clearly are teaching mostly to the Generation Y/Millennials in our Childbirth Education settings. They have not known a world without computers. Yet, they are preparing for a normal, natural life event that will probably happen spontaneously at a non-precise time with an unpredictable timeline. These Millennials have had much exposure, and possibly overexposure, to PowerPoint. They probably "learned" from it in most of their upper grades through high school and college, and in work-related responsibilities, meetings, and conferences. Therefore, many of your class participants associate PowerPoint with learning and sharing information. They may expect the same in your childbirth education class. To them, it's just another class, and not preparation for a significant life event—one that requires a great deal of hands-on physical and emotional support. They need to develop the confidence that the expectant mother's body knows what to do, hopefully with our direct influence. Can graphics and words shown on a computer screen accomplish this? That is for you, as the educator, to decide the effectiveness in using PowerPoint in your childbirth education classes, as well as your comfort level for effective teaching. What can you accomplish with its use that you cannot without it?

If the PowerPoint appears to be more of a focus for the educator than the learner, then learner detachment may occur. Once the possible detachment takes place, it can be difficult for the educator and learner to reverse this process, and learning could be diminished, instead of enhanced.

You are best qualified to choose this as a strategy in your curriculum design. You may have created your own, or have access to a PowerPoint created or purchased by the facility in which you teach. That should be an option for you. I trust educators to decide which methods will best enhance the type of class they teach, and be most effective with their teaching styles and other strategies they use to maximize learning.

It can, indeed, be a challenge to keep this Generation Y/ Millennial, and sometimes Generation X, participants engaged when they are used to getting so much information digitally, and want fast and immediate processing and results. It is enlightening and interesting to observe when they realize that childbirth is not going to be any of the above. That some of the information they received online is misinformation, and that they will need to use their bodies, not their computers, for this life-altering experience, and without a specific schedule on their electronic device.

Are we just showing and telling information, or are we teaching hands-on life skills, or are we trying to integrate both? Is a laptop (or whatever system is used) going to be most helpful when the laboring mother needs significant counter pressure on her back and hips? Will it be more effective and relevant to show fetal descent and rotation through active images within a PowerPoint? Will the relevance increase to hand a teaching pelvis and fetal model to the expectant parents to problem-solve and work as partners to "open" the pelvis and rotate the baby through? If PowerPoint is skillfully utilized, it can summarize content, enhance visuals, and require fewer charts. But it needs to be balanced with many other strategies so that it is not the complete instructional part of your class. It must be used appropriately so that your back is not to the class, and that you are not just "reading" to your adult learners, or they may very well tune out to "just another class." Recently, I received two comments from Millennials, on separate evaluations, that are worth mentioning:

> "Having a conversational class vs. PowerPoint was perfect."

> "Thank you for not using PowerPoint. It helped my learning tremendously."

Another activity you may want to do for yourself is also included: "An Educator in My Life." Most of us have had impactful experiences with role models and mentors in our lives. This reflective process may help you to verbalize and incorporate these transformational experiences into your own teaching.

Your curriculum will continue to evolve, not only with updated information, but as you stretch and grow, not only as a lifelong learner, but as a responsible educator, keeping yourself fresh, enthusiastic, interesting, and credible. However, teaching is not all about you imparting information. It only feels that way at times.

Become who you need to be with a tremendous amount of adaptability for yourself and class participants, but be true to yourself. Find that balance of knowledge, resources, and caring about your participants. Accept and validate their needs and ideas (see the Adult Learners section). As an example, I have admired more tattoos and piercings, tying those in with coping strategies, as well as the unique pillows, mats, and bags that have been brought to classes.

You notice, care, and reinforce the value of their presence. Balance your comfort level with what may be outside the box in order to reach that challenging, but wonderful diversity of learners that come to every class. Personally, it took me a bit of time to find comfort in leading "pelvic rockers" and position changes, as well as movement to achieve those position changes to songs, ranging anywhere from Tina Turner to AC/DC, with tremendous participation, I might add, and much laughter, which is a great relaxant. What teachable moments these are!

Speaking of laughter, humor is funny! It helps your partici-pants relax, feel more at ease, and they are more likely to enjoy your classes. Some class members arrive ready to have a fun time in class. Many, however, are unsure, and even fear the idea of laboring and giving birth, but are aware enough to attend your classes. Early on in class, I will ask the group if they have thought of labor and birth as being fun. (Watching their reactions provides laughter and humor for me.) Then I ask if they consider bringing this baby into their family unit, and into the world, a reason for celebration. Of course, they unanimously agree. I follow that with asking them, "How do you celebrate without having fun?" It gets them every time, relaxes them, and many begin to see that this could be a fun experience, especially with some insight and preparation.

On a recent talk show, a very famous, seasoned, and amazing actor could barely put two of his own sentences together in the interview. It didn't even come close to how engaging he is in his movies. What does that tell us? Even though we think we need to follow the "script" of our curriculum plans, we are not actors (although it may feel as if we are, or need to be, at times). We transport the knowledge and skills that equal empowerment to those who seek us out, and we need flexibility. What a tremendous responsibility as we are still being the "miracle workers," "multi-taskers," "educators," "entertainers," and "caretakers," while being true to ourselves. Believe in yourself, but temper it with complete humility.

AN EDUCATOR OR EDUCATORS IN MY LIFE

What has made this person or people memorable in your life?

_____

_____

_____

What stands out about this person or persons?

_____

_____

_____

What qualities did he/she/they have?

_____

_____

_____

How did he/she/they make you feel?

_____

_____

_____

What will you always remember as a Life Lesson that you have carried from your experience?

_____

_____

_____

How would you thank her/him/them?

_____

_____

_____

Considerations for Additional Teaching Strategies

- ◉ Create your own interactive, evidence-based curriculum plan that promotes safe, natural, and healthy pregnancies, births, breastfeeding, and postpartum experiences.

- ◉ Examine your motives honestly. Are you absolutely sure you know where you stand on everything before teaching it as the "expert?" Or is teaching the beginning of the erosion of our objectivity in presenting options, not the beginning of expertise? Find the truth of your objectivity.

- ◉ Also, as previously mentioned, help parents find the joy in this life-changing experience, and prepare with an abundance of meaningful communication.

Hopefully, you have noticed a number of spiraling examples between this section and the information presented about Adult Learning.

EDUCATE YOURSELF AND OTHERS

Create your own environment

Omit concerns

Make yourself the expert

Movement

Unify your skills

Nullify the fear

Increase your confidence

Cooperate with your style

Align your thoughts

Take ownership

Invite your spirit

Obey your soul

Number your priorities

Trust in yourself

Recognize your skills

Understand yourself

Support yourself

Trust in your support

Program Evaluations

The term "evaluation" is an important one for childbirth educators in many ways. For instance, as lifelong learners, and because we care so much, we are regularly looking at the content, its flow, and our strategies in our curriculum designs to either update the information, freshen it, or vary it because we may teach it so often. These are qualities of a conscientious educator.

As mentioned in the Curriculum Design section of The Fundamentals of Teaching, evaluation is essential in assessing the efficacy of the Learner Objectives we have described that are the essence of our teaching. Some suggested strategies to accomplish this could include:

- Educator observation
- Discussion
- Follow-up review
- Handout answers
- Question/Answer
- Return demonstration
- Homework assignments
- Participant sharing/reporting out
- Or simply asking them directly whether the objective was met

Another facet of evaluation is Performance Evaluations if you work as a hospital employee. This is discussed under the Hospital-Based Childbirth Education section in the Professional Practice chapter. Participant evaluations can be useful to the educator, if they are relevant and the appropriate length. If you teach at a hospital or other facility, those facilities usually have an accountability tool.

Most occupations do not require an employee to be actively evaluated each time they go to work. This, however, is part of the process of childbirth education. Many private educators use participant evaluations as well. Of course, we value class participants' feedback from an educational point of view, as well as for patient satisfaction for the facility. Satisfaction with the class, educator, and facility are important.

There are several areas to consider when composing an effective evaluation tool. I've helped put together evaluation ideas for a number of facilities. Considerations should include:

- What are you seeking with the evaluation?
- What will be done with this information?
- How is the feedback going to be helpful to the educator?
- How will this information be helpful to a facility?
- Did the participants feel valued and able to ask questions?
- Was the information relevant and useful?
- Were there opportunities to learn skills, and options to prepare for labor and birth, as well as for informed decision-making?

The format of the evaluation can impact the results. It should be short, and easy to read and understand. Three to five simple statements can be enough. Feedback can get fuzzy, and perhaps "watered down," if an evaluation gets up to 10 to 12 statements or questions. Participants may lose focus on the original and basic purpose of the evaluation. If an evaluation number scale is used three or four being the maximum, that would be enough for helpful and meaningful feedback. More could be confusing. If words are used, some guidelines should follow, such as three to four choices. Open-ended choices are not as useful, but a short space for follow-up comments may provide helpful information.

The choices should be positive, constructive, and directly related to relevance and participation opportunities, as previously mentioned. Questions or statements that concern teaching style, time management, and what could be improved with content or instruction are generally not as relevant for active, accurate feedback. Most participants are not fully qualified to give an academic evaluation or assessment, but they are usually very clear as to the value of the class for them and their significance in the class. For instance, they may not have the background to evaluate educational soundness of your program, and strategies we use to maximize learning. For example, a participant may not recognize how spiraling reinforced learning, and looks at it as just repetition. Also, improvement questions, or statement opportunities given at the end, could indicate some concern or issue that participants have not expressed or asked about. How valuable would this information be after the fact? If the evaluator feels this really needs to be sought out, then a mid-series or mid-class mini evaluation could be completed for possible rectification purposes that could help both educator and participant. An improvement question at the very end also implies that this class offering must need improvement, and is not the best that can be offered.

In rare cases, it could be an outlet for participants to vent an issue that is not directly related to the class, educator, or possibly facility, thus not a productive bit of information for accurate feedback. Getting direct contradictory feedback from participants can also be perplexing to process, such as "too much practice," "not enough practice," "understood my options," "did not fully understand my options," "wanted to see video clips," "didn't want to see video clips," and so on.

When you distribute the evaluation forms can also impact the accuracy of feedback you are seeking. For instance, giving participants an evaluation to complete right at the ending time of class almost guarantees that you will not receive thoughtful feedback from participants, and will cause them to stay after.

Including the evaluation in their folder of initial handouts, and reviewing it as you review others, can be much more helpful, as well as finishing a few minutes early. Allowing time for more relaxed, thoughtful feedback is much more effective.

Since educators get so used to this process, and reading the results and know they did a great job, gave it their all, and were well-prepared, why can we be so hard on ourselves? For instance, out of an example of 20 evaluations, we may get 19 glowing and wonderful evaluations, and one "iffy" one. We may then obsess, possibly feel defensive and hurt, and allow ourselves to briefly go into "failure mode" over the one "iffy" one, even when we know better. As much as you care and prepare, do not allow rare criticism to make you feel as if you have not done your best—or even failed. We are so passionate about what we teach, and want others to gain so much, it can be difficult. Please put it in perspective and know, that given the sheer numbers and the vast differences in human nature, that there will always be those participants who will never give positive evaluations, or ever appreciate all that you have taught and provided, and all that they have learned. If, of course, you notice a pattern of evaluation scores or comments that do warrant attention, then humbly examine your curriculum design and strategies to see what might need to be done. Therefore, for the many reasons stated in this section, it is most beneficial to all to have the appropriate evaluation to get the best and most useful information that can be accurately used.

Birth Plans: Informed Decision-Making

Birth Plans have significantly evolved into a much more effective teaching and communication tool for choices in birth. Historically, they potentially became sources of frustration for all involved, as well as possible annoyances. There are many factors that have contributed to this change.

- Evidence-based information and practices

- Updated ACOG guidelines that now encourage low-risk laboring women to stay home longer

- Our teaching has become more than just telling, and is allowing expectant couples to truly internalize the choice factor and own their experience more authentically, thus using informed decision-making with a deeper under-standing of personal options.

- This process has become more than just a list of possible things that might get to happen. With increased ownership comes confidence and effective communication among the couple and with the providers.

- Empowerment and flexibility can go hand-in-hand in the labor/birth experience, and that is more keenly understood.

Ownership of their experience has also increased with choices of the name of their Birth Plan, as well as the type/format they prefer to use that fits the style of learning, decision-making, and communicating that will best suit the expectant couple. There are several possible names that are used for Birth Plans, and that list continues to grow. These include:

- Birth Wishes

- Birth Preferences

- Personal Plan for Birth

- Birth Design
- Birth by Design
- My Birth

These choices in wording immediately imply the personal power of choice, which is further reinforced by the choice of source and format choices, including:

- A checklist. Some hospitals provide this, and it could also be taken from the book used in class, or created by the couple.
- A checklist couples create with space for further explanation of their choice or choices.
- "Shop" for one on the internet that feels relevant and appealing.
- All narrative that could include their philosophies of birth and descriptions of their choices.
- A small piece of paper with some affirmations
- A few key thoughts, but not necessarily written

Recently, I had an expectant woman in my class who shared that her Birth Design was the thought, "I will move a lot and will know what to do." She was expressing her confidence, and fully understood the use of an option that was going to work for her, and that this did not need to be a formal, written document.

I offer an option called Birth Power Plan that couples can either complete using a list or narrative format to express their preferences. It also includes an "arrangements" section not often thought of, or seen, in other possible formats, and encourages planning for before and after that may not have been readily considered. The example of this is provided.

It can be relevant and helpful to allow some time in class for participants to start with some ideas of options, title, and format, as well as allowing opportunities for sharing and networking. This can also be given as a specific assignment. Couples should have enough information about the normalcy of birth, and the effectiveness of evidence-based comfort strategies, possible impacts of interventions, and the fact that their provider facilitates and supports their birth. In addition to understanding this process, and completing the chosen plan in advance, some hospitals now offer and encourage a scheduled meeting or consultation with a birth professional to discuss their plan, complete pre-registration, and ask questions about any other topics in advance of their birth experiences.

Thankfully, previous topics/procedures that, on occasion, had to be negotiated are now routine. Some examples include intermittent fetal monitoring with low-risk laboring patients, not using pain medication, freedom of movement, skin to skin, and no separation of mother and baby, to name a few. The midwifery model of care is now much more prevalent in many hospitals. This meaningful process has, indeed, become a most helpful, but flexible, form of communication among couples and with their providers.

BIRTH POWER PLAN

Contractions:

_____

_____

_____

_____

_____

_____

_____

Arrangements:

(pack, house, pets, pre-registration, insurance, baby items, labor support)

_____

_____

_____

_____

_____

_____

Medications:

No _____

Yes _____

Maybe _____

Positions:

Other notes:

Self-Care for the Educator

We are in the most incredible, giving field, in so many ways. As previously mentioned, we are the "caretakers of the world," the people pleasers, sharing our passions about such an abundance of wonderful information that can absolutely help so many prepare for an incredible and life-altering event. We are inspiring, caring educators, and reinforcers of life-skills. We want to be responsible for everyone's happiness in our classes, and sometimes, their learning. We work hard to have a solid curriculum to meet all types of learners. We balance and update our information. We are aware of hospital policies. We teach comfort and communication skills that are potentially new to participants. We encourage and teach informed decision-making, sometimes even negotiation skills. They are the consumers, after all, who have registered and paid for your class and sought out your information. It all sounds pretty wonderful, right? It certainly can be, but all of this has some very realistic pitfalls if we do not take precautions to take care of ourselves. These pitfalls can include:

⊚ We try to please people who could never be pleased. Hopefully, we rarely see these people in our classes, or sometimes, evaluation results. This can be a toxic draw to our energy unless we hold our heads high, treating them as kindly and with as much respect as everyone else. Sometimes they may be scared or, find it challenging to be in a group, or just take a while to get to know. Sometimes not (see Adult Learning).

⊚ How do we overall choose to expend our energy? Even high energy can be easily depleted if we allow it. Most classes energize us, but let's be real—not all. Balancing your curriculum is not only for optimal learning and engaging individuals, but it should be for us to balance our energy as well. Educators must continually multitask in their classes, and this can be exhausting.

⊚ With some groups, we may feel as if we are convincing them more than teaching them, another potential energy-zapper.

⊚ With some individuals, the educated and informed caretaker in us feels like we are trying to save them from their own decisions, still another energy-zapper.

⊚ We have all taught through exhaustion, illness, ill family members, and many other life challenges. More energy gone.

⊚ Are you a birth junkie, research junkie, curriculum junkie, or any other type of related junkie? Is it energizing for you? Determine that and, be truthful with yourself. Even positive addictions can be exhausting. Several years ago, some newer instructors and I were talking with Penny Simkin who, even at that time, was so very accomplished. As many of you know, her original professional background was in physical therapy, and she shared with us that at the beginning of her childbirth education career, she was "an awful teacher" (hard to believe), and that she had to work 40 to 50 hours a week to learn the obstetrical and maternity care information to teach the next class! I was not sure whether to feel shocked, impressed, amazed, or saddened, and probably felt a bit of each. Luckily, she shared that she was good on comfort measures, but I was wondering how she even had the energy to teach at that time!

In addition to the above insight regarding energy, here are some specific considerations for your teaching:

⊚ Stay hydrated and take sips as you are teaching.

⊚ Have a good, nutritious meal before class. You will figure out the best timing of that meal with your teaching.

- Take a break for yourself when you give a break. You do not have to spend your entire break with participants. You can find ways to have your own break during a class break. Find a restroom and a place to just sit, even for just a moment, that is not generally used by class participants, but is still conveniently close. Set limits on your availability for breaks by doing that from the very beginning.

- What if a couple unexpectedly shows up 30 minutes early? Certainly, greet and welcome them, but do not feel as if you have to play "hostess" during your precious prep time. They can read through materials, go get a beverage or snack, and will be completely fine.

- What are your feelings and circumstances if a couple asks you to attend their labor and birth which, of course, usually means being on call. Be honest with yourself. As much as you would probably love to be there, will that work for you and your life circumstances? I have attended close to 280 births, having only been on call about 10 of those times. The rest have worked out seeing them at the hospital when I am there anyways, and many times running into them while doing tours of the units.

- Do you keep records, and make your own postpartum calls or visits? Again, this is completely up to you and your life experiences, especially if you are volunteering your time. This also pertains to reunions. Even if someone else volunteers to organize it, attendance could be on your own time, whether you teach privately or in a hospital, as it seems as if fewer and fewer hospitals are funding reunions.

- You may have found other ways of preserving your energy and self-care while teaching. I generally arrive early, set-up, then take a short walk, using some nice, slow breathing to clear my head and calm my nerves, even though I have been teaching a very long time, each class is a new adventure with different characteristics.

⊙ Please use the wonderful life skills that we embrace and teach others for yourself. Why do we so easily forget the benefits of relaxation, focusing, massage, and slow breathing when it comes to taking care of ourselves?

⊙ Drop the chains often, and have other completely different components and interests in your lives. Add more fun, including dancing.

⊙ Stand in truth with yourself and embrace self-care. Find the balance of protecting and sharing your energy.

⊙ Even with this wonderfully fabulous profession, burnout can burn you to the core.

I strongly encourage you to study and complete the two enclosed sheets for yourself. You are wonderful, and we all want you to recharge that powerful energy of yours. How often do we see this type of personal information about self-care as childbirth educators in training handbooks or guides, books, and in workshops? Certainly not enough.

Yoga Nidra: Interview with Karen Brody of Bold Tranquility

Many will recognize the name Karen Brody from the *Birth* play. As playwright, Karen based the play on her interviews with over 100 mothers. The play has been performed in numerous communities worldwide since 2006. *Birth* has certainly contributed to the conversation around physiologic birth, improving childbirth for mothers and babies, and raising awareness.

Karen's work with Yoga Nidra comes from personal experience with feeling and acting "crazypants." All humans can relate to those feelings. Our society defines success as getting the most accomplished, and does not focus on rest and inner peace. Karen does.

From an interview, Karen told Connie, "Yoga Nidra is a guided pathway to deep rest/sleep. It is so simple. Who doesn't want to rest? Physicians, midwives, nurses, doulas, childbirth-educators: they could all be classified as shift workers with odd hours (on call). Even when a doula is anticipating a call from a client, this messes up circadian rhythms. You cannot get the rest you so richly deserve. After all, humans are meant to follow the sunrise, sunset, and moonrise. It can be difficult for these professionals."

Yoga Nidra is not indulgent, and we should not feel guilty taking a break. We know that pushing ourselves in our personal and professional lives leads to stress, tension, and other physical symptoms, including adrenal fatigue, weight gain, acceleration of the aging process, and so much more. With Yoga Nidra, you can obtain a feeling of well-being, and halt the production of cortisol and anxiety-producing hormones.

Yoga Nidra is dynamic, and helps you to welcome all feelings, including pain, and clears nerve pathways to the brain. So, this makes Yoga Nidra especially beneficial for laboring mothers in seeking a physiologic birth, and for postpartum/nursing mothers. It helps women to seek the wisdom and the quiet sanctuary of their innermost thoughts, coordinate all of the baggage we bring to each experience, and find the true self. What about for childbirth educators?

To practice, Yoga Nidra, professionals might lie flat, on a yoga mat, on your back with palms up. With eyes closed, take several slow, relaxed breaths. Focus on how the breath feels when you inhale and exhale. Begin by focusing attention on your foot, visualizing each toe of each foot. Move upward on your foot, to your heel, calf, knee, thigh, hip of one leg, and do the same for the other leg. Then take your attention to the pelvic area, abdomen, stomach, and chest, continuing slow, rhythmic breathing. Now take your attention to hand/fingers, forearm, elbow and shoulder, and do the same for the other side. Move then to your neck, jaw, face, and to the top of your head. Rest there for a moment and enjoy relaxation! If you've not fallen asleep, it is time to come back to the room. Become aware of where you are, and open your eyes!

What is the difference between meditation and Yoga Nidra? Yoga Nidra is a guided meditation, and you go into a deep, relaxing, sleepy state. Meditation is in an upright position, and does not promote sleeping. With Yoga Nidra, you rest in awareness.

Want to learn more about Yoga Nidra? Download the free Bold Tranquility App – Meditation, Mindfulness, Sleep by Squat Productions from the iTunes store (at the time of publishing this *app was not available for Android or Google Play devices). Go to www.irest.us and purchase* some of the practices of iRest Yoga Nidra.

For Further Reading

Brody, K. (2011). My body rocks. *Mothering Magazine, March/April.* 36-43.

Eastman-Mueller, H. et al. (2013). iRest (Integrative Restoration) Yoga Nidra on the College Campus: Changes in stress, depression, worry and mindfulness. *International Journal of Yoga Therapy, 23,* 15-24.

Kim, S.D. (2014). Effects of yoga exercises of life stress and blood glucose levels in nursing students. *Journal of Physical Therapy Science, 26*(12), 2003-2006.

Stankovic, L. (2011) Transforming trauma: A qualitative feasibility study of integrative restoration Yoga Nidra on combat-related post-traumatic stress disorder. *International Journal of Yoga Therapy, 21,* 23-37

THE CONFIDENT EDUCATOR...

Opens the eyes and hearts of learners,
Is a life-long learner,
Values each individual,
Values each group,
Is open to differing viewpoints,
Welcomes feedback,
Learns from the students and their experiences,
Allows learning to happen for all.

"If we all did the things we are really capable of doing,
we would literally astound ourselves."
– Thomas Edison

What gifts do you have to make you a wonderful educator?

_____

_____

_____

_____

_____

What might be challenging for you?

_____

_____

_____

_____

_____

_____

BALANCE AND RELAX!!

"Have you ever been too busy driving to stop for gas?"
– Stephen Covey

⊚ Balance of the spirit, body, and soul is key.

⊚ Take time for you!

⊚ Clear the way– always keep the path to your heart open.

⊚ Do for yourself more than what you would do for others!

⊚ If you become your job, you lose you.

⊚ There is power in balancing your lives and truly caring for yourself!

⊚ Do what helps you to live a full life.

⊚ Eliminate the stresses you have control over and add the comforts.

⊚ Redefine your priorities, if that is what you need.

⊚ Create time for yourself.

PROGRESSIVE RELAXATION FOR YOU

⊚ Comfortable position and environment

⊚ Deep cleansing breaths

⊚ Self-body check: move down to follow the natural path of relaxation– top of head, face, neck, shoulders, arms, hands, back, chest, abdomen, bottom, thighs, calves, feet

⊚ One to five minutes daily minimum

ADDITIONAL ACTIVITIES FOR YOU

⊚ Head rolls and front arm stretches with breaths

⊚ Self-massage: temples, jawline, shoulders, feet

⊚ Play

⊚ Train massage

⊚ Promise to yourself: small steps, not resolution!

Follow your promises and follow yourself. You are too important to be taken too seriously. While you are so serious with yourself, facts, others, etc., the soul train leaves the station without you!

Take care of yourself!

CHAPTER 6

The Professional Practice: Foxtrot to Jazz

Where an educator chooses to teach classes can greatly depend on the geographical area and services available. For instance, an urban area may have many hospitals and services compared to a smaller, less-populated, or rural area. It may also depend on available opportunities and/or personal preference. Some urban areas may have privately owned centers or facilities that offer classes. There are advantages and possible disadvantages to any of these settings.

Whether you are teaching in a hospital or private setting, it is vital that you are aware of and follow the standards, code of ethics, expectations, and guidelines of your earned certification.

Hospital-Based Childbirth Education

Most hospitals or facilities that offer obstetrics offer childbirth education and other prenatal classes. Professional advantages of a hospital setting could include having a classroom/conference room in which to teach, room set-up and cleaning, provision of teaching tools, and visuals, such as charts, video segments, an audio-visual system, class registration, marketing, and regular income. There is also the labor and delivery, and mother/baby units for tours and reference to use comfort strategies. The educator may be better acquainted with the obstetrical providers that participants see for their care. This also provides more direct opportunities to be acquainted with, and obtain updates from the nursing staff and providers. Be visible on the units. Talk to the staff. Always get direct clearance for tours.

It can also be helpful to set up interviews, if needed or desired, with charge nurses, obstetrical and anesthesia providers, and postpartum staff. This enhances communication, and shows your interest in what they do and in the patients you share, and information and comfort strategies that you teach. Maintain that connection to enhance mutual understanding. You may also have that opportunity if hospital employees are in your classes.

Historically, teaching hospital-based childbirth education presented challenges of incorporating our curriculum of optimal ways to give birth, but in a medical setting that included routine medical procedures and policies. Then, evidence-based practices and updated ACOG guidelines rocked our worlds and closed many of the potential gaps between our teaching and maternity care, both based on these practices and guidelines. The more well-known ones include induction and increasing the dilation consideration of the Early-Labor phase. We can provide resources and evidence-based information without perceived biases, which has resulted in expectant parents being more informed and confident to ask relevant questions, and provide birth plans, wishes, or designs. Parents are equipped with comfort strategies that are evidence-based, and are making a difference with hospital births. This has allowed maternal satisfaction and patient satisfaction to be complementary.

Hospital education, in many cases, can potentially allow expectant parents to feel more connected and involved with their facilities, thus providing connections between what they learn in class and what they experience in their hospital labors and births, with empowerment and understanding.

Choosing which hospital to teach at will likely be limited by where openings exist. However, make sure that it is a facility where you will be proud to be part of the staff, where the parent-education department is highly respected, and you are in agreement with the values of the hospital, as well as the curriculum and procedures for your department. For example, if there is a required curriculum, find out why, and be comfortable that you can add your own touches (as previously discussed in the Curriculum Design section), and feel flexible with it. Some programs will provide handouts. Some combine their handouts with your own. And some may have you provide all of your own handouts, and have the resources to make or receive copies.

If a PowerPoint is a required part of your teaching, be sure you have a clear understanding as to the motives regarding this requirement. As a Parent Education Coordinator, I trust that the certified educators on staff know what will work best for what they are teaching. They are only asked to submit their teaching outline, handouts, and PowerPoint slides if they have chosen to create one for my review. Ask to see the class evaluation form that you will be distributing and submitting so that you are clear regarding the areas in which you will be evaluated, as well as what is valued by the hospital for employed educators. It is also helpful to review the Performance Evaluation process and ask to see the form(s). Since this is related to your employment, find out the basis of this performance evaluation that your supervisor will be annually completing, possibly with your input. Does it feel fair and balanced? Does it include your role in the performance standards of the hospital, and your job description and responsibilities? If, for example, your Performance Evaluation is based primarily on the class evaluations you receive, the scope may feel rather limited, especially as an employee and part of the hospital. Your comfort and understanding is of utmost importance.

Employee responsibilities will also, generally, include completion of online Healthstream modules, possible staff and general meetings, maintaining professional certifications, health screenings, annual flu shots, current BLS (CPR) certification, keeping up with a professional hospital email account, reporting to a supervisor, and agreeing with the hospital's possible mission statement, visions, and values. These expectations will most likely differ if you have contractor versus employee status.

Find your joy and freedom within your hospital teaching setting. Be your own champion. This is a unique job situation where you are self-directed, but working as a supported team player. Embracing the facility communication, flexibility, and insight is key. Stay informed. Many hospitals will go through reinvention phases, which can be challenging, but look at the big picture as improvements.

In your hospital teaching, there are too many variable and individual situations to always find clarity, and even expect transformation in what you believe. But you will speak the evidence-based truth in a fair way to patients, staff, and providers. Your positive approach will be contagious. Encourage participants to empowerment and awareness of options, and you can help expectant parents to find their own joy and satisfaction in their hospital labor and birth experiences.

Private or Community-Based Teaching

This became a challenging section to address, as there are many options and directions with which to go, which is something you would need to figure out first for yourself. In the field of childbirth education, it is essential to examine the birth culture, and demographics of your geographical area, to determine the following:

- Is this area hospital-saturated, and do most of them have

a Parent Education program?

- Would a private educator be used and able to succeed as a business?

- What settings are available that interest me?

- Is there a church, community center, or free-standing Birth Center where I could independently teach?

- Are there private facilities or businesses that offer classes?

- Would I teach in my home or go privately to clients' homes?

- Is there an individual provider who would be open to their own educator, or any other possibilities?

These last questions could drive everything in getting started:

- What do I plan to offer, staying within the scope of my certification? How would that fit into my chosen setting?

- How does teaching privately benefit me considering setting preferences, philosophy, flexibility, finances, and scheduling? Look at your motives carefully and be realistic with them as marketing. Succeeding could potentially be much more challenging in many ways.

- Interview other private educators, or ones who have done this in the past, in your area.

- Decide if you prefer teaching completely independently or within a facility. (Go back to the "available settings" question.)

- You may want to "shop" for a business advisor to get started, or take a local class or workshop about getting started.

If you want to start a business, you will need to consider the following:

- Where would my clients come from?

- Find out what the area hospitals offer and charge to help

you determine what to offer and what to charge. Consider within this realm, and for part of your marketing offering, specials, or package deals.

Create a business plan that includes:

- Business or trade name, and file the proper application for your county.
- Will your business be a sole proprietorship, partnership, limited liability company (LLC), or corporation? Do your homework and be clear on each of these choices, and what the benefits and liabilities are, as well as what paperwork needs to be filed. This is where professional advice can be most helpful.
- Create a mission statement that determines the majority of your decisions and helps with your marketing.
- Budget for possible rent (if any), marketing, teaching and business materials, and other costs, depending how the business is set up: a separate phoneline, for example.
- Consider your insurance needs.

Marketing plans and considerations can make or break your business:

- How will you present yourself? (Remember your mission statement.)
- Brochures? Cards? How will you design them and where will you put them?
- Social Media
  - Making a Facebook Business page?
  - Creating a blog?
  - Using Twitter?

- Networking on other sites?
- Creating a website where clients can reach you?
- Listing yourself in a local directory service?
- Combining social media for a strong presence?

Having a social-media plan can help you to determine how clients will reach you, register, and pay you, if this will be needed for the structure of your business. Here are some other considerations.

- What is your timeframe and guidelines to make this work?
- Do you realistically have the funding to make this work?
- How far do you want to go, procedurally and financially, to make this a business?
- How motivated are you to make the time to build this business, and keep up with the social-media presence and updates?
- What would the numbers need to be to hold or cancel a class?
- What materials do you need in which to start? Where could they be stored?
- Are you prepared for an inconsistent income, or no income, from this endeavor for an unpredictable time?
- Will you need, and be able to have, an accountant to keep track of finances and timely submission of tax documents?
- Do you really want to teach in addition to having the responsibility of being a business owner?
- Many educators are surprised and overwhelmed about the amount of work it takes to start a business, maintain it, and succeed at it. Again, so much depends on your area and the needs of the community, as well as the effectiveness of your

marketing. There are no guarantees, and some educators have given it their best shot, but then realized that the business world has caused their passion for birth and teaching to dwindle, and it is not for them. Just as in birth classes, we encourage empowerment, knowledge of options, trying many things, and doing what works for you and your interests and circumstances.

Evaluating Research for Incorporation into Childbirth Education Classes

Since much of our childbirth education curriculum is based on current evidence and evidence-based practices, it is important that we use research wisely and give expectant parents accurate information. Research will be the basis for helping participants understand the process of labor and birth, gain confidence in their experiences, and understand the significance of their options.

To use research, childbirth educators need to understand research practices enough so they can learn and to incorporate it within their teaching. You are a valuable resource to give class participants accurate information preparing for this life-changing event, and allowing more optimal participation in class, as well as communication with providers. Working as a team with consistent information between participants, educators, and providers encourages more effective experiences for all.

When you understand the standards, scope of practice, and code of ethics of your professional certification, it will further reinforce your need to accurately use research in your educational setting. Your professional standards dictate that you incorporate current research into the classes. Staying objective and balanced with research can be challenging. Sometimes, research findings can be manipulated.

Many educators peruse detailed research on a regular basis. They find it enlightening and enjoyable. Others may not. It can be overwhelming and challenging to not only understand, but to decipher whether a study is valid, and then decide how to incorporate it as an expert resource in classes. When seeking out research for personal and teaching use, you may get frustrated when reading research journals as the findings can be reported in a highly technical format. This format makes it hard to understand the findings, let alone find practical ways of using the findings in childbirth education curriculum.

You can access research in several ways to help you stay current. One is to use the Cochrane Library, which is published by the Cochrane Collaboration, an independent non-profit organization, which is updated every three months. Abstracts and summaries of systematic reviews are available at no cost. An abstract is an introductory summary that discusses the purpose of the study, statement of purpose, and sometimes how the findings were determined. A systematic review is a compilation of relevant studies regarding one clinical topic that are presented in a balanced and impartial fashion. Sometimes this term is interchangeably used with the term meta-analysis, where the results of multiple independent studies are combined and statistically presented. If a full systematic review is desired, rather than a summary, that can be accessed if a subscription is acquired.

The quality of a research study is directly related to its reliability. Watch for the following characteristics in the study you are evaluating:

- The researcher's qualifications, affiliations, and funding sources.

- The credibility of the publication.

- How the reported results are organized. Are they easy to follow, and are the actual results easy to find?

- Accuracy of the research study title. Does it reflect what the purpose of the study is, and the reported results?

- What methods are used? Does the sampling seem objective, as well as the reported results?

- Is the research clear and supported?

- Are the explanations, processes, and conclusions clear and logical?

- Are the research and conclusions relevant to the original topic and field of study?

- Are the conclusions logical and documented with a clear support of the findings?

Manipulation of findings and numbers can sometimes be part of a research project where the findings and numbers can be rationalized to appear to support the original premise. Also, look for selective/partial reporting of information and motivation behind that. This may especially be used in advertising claims, or in ways to seek funding/grants for organizations or projects.

Methods of collecting information are also available in possibly more accessible ways, such as newsletters from childbirth-education organizations, and links from other birth organizations, reliable webpages, and AGOG guidelines for various topics. Much research contributes to these guidelines, and they are relatively easy to access. However, some topics, such as the timing of umbilical cord clamping post-birth, may give a "committee opinion," with a fair amount of supportive research included, yet it still has not been proven or established.

Another topic that has much research backing, yet seems to continue to stay in the controversial area, is safety of oral intake (drinking and eating) during labor, although ACOG's Committee Opinion does state that modest amounts of clear liquids might be appropriate in low-risk labors, but shares that there is not enough evidence regarding potential surgical fasting periods for any solids. Thus, this can create a dilemma of what to share in class. Back to the use of valid research and, possibly, what are perceived as controversial topics, in a childbirth education setting. Be informed, but also be prepared to address questions and concerns, and find ways to incorporate a balance of information that is fair and relevant to the participants, while staying within the scope of your practice and ethics.

Social Media

For Me, My Teaching, or Both?

As previously discussed in the section on PowerPoint, the childbearing population have not known a world without computers. This means that social media plays a major role in their existence. There are numerous opportunities to find evidence-based information at a moment's notice, and direct ways to encourage class participants to see first-hand opinions and guidelines from major and reputable organizations, especially looking for websites that end with .org, .edu, and .gov. These can also be used as points of discussion in class, as well as individual discussions with their provider:

- ACOG – American College of Obstetrics and Gynecologist, primarily the Committee Opinions are specific topics
- AWHONN – Association of Women's Health, Obstetric and Neonatal Nurses

- Cochrane Library – Database of systematic reviews
- ACNM – American College of Nurse Midwives
- DONA – International Doula Organization
- WHO – World Health Organization
- NIH – National Institutes of Health under Women's Health
- Childbirth Connection
- CIMS – Coalition for Improving Maternity Services

You may have many other sources you recommend to your classes. The above is designed to be a very basic go-to list for quick, valid information, helping class participants avoid the possibilities of unfiltered misinformation that can occur with random Googling. Additional sources that may take more time and involvement could be journals, blogs, articles, online forums, and professional experts. You may have experienced some classes quickly bonded and set up private Facebook pages or email groups.

More than likely, social media may not be a major teaching strategy in your prepared childbirth curriculum. Time, class preferences, and your personal preference and comfort level may dictate the extent of its use. It may, however, be a further consideration for your professional use and possible exposure. There are many participatory venues available, beginning with professional memberships that can lead to myriad opportunities and connections, including business accounts. There are many to choose from, which entails your own searches.

As a childbirth educator, I'd recommend joining at least one, or all three major organizations: Lamaze International, ICEA, and CAPPA. Lamaze International has an *LCCE Educator Social Media Guide,* and ICEA has a social media position paper, both of which can provide helpful information and considerations as a professional. All have informational websites.

Since it was previously mentioned that this wonderful profession can be rather isolating, networking becomes even more critical to not only share ideas, but to get news, updates, and see others' perspectives. As we are educating and empowering others, we need to do that for ourselves. There are so many opportunities and venues available that it becomes necessary to narrow it down to what is most relevant and helpful for you, the time you have to invest, and your intent to create a public presence that you must regularly update. If your goal includes public presence in the community, and you teach for a hospital setting, be aware of any guidelines and conflicts of interest, especially with business accounts.

Networking and obtaining recertification contact hours through social media, and narrowing it down to what is personally manageable, can help us all to branch out, obtain ideas for content and teaching strategies, create our own presence, build bridges, and obtain information and validation for what we are doing in cost-effective ways. Of course, attending workshops, conferences, and reading current books for childbirth educators are also very helpful to balance out your connections. Whether as an educator or expectant parent, we need to be cognizant of the fact that it comes back to the body knowing and accomplishing what technology cannot, and to help parents obtain that perspective.

AFTERWORD

Writing this book has been a phenomenal journey, with a full and grateful heart, even through the loss of my co-author, Connie, and my beloved, supportive furry creature, Laz. This is not really a conclusion, but a continued encouragement. Childbirth education is a calling, and is both a privilege and pleasure. Depending on your circumstances, teaching childbirth preparation may feel, at times, isolating. Please network personally as much as possible, whether locally, nationally, or internationally. There is nothing like feeling the energy, passion, and participation at a conference, with several hundred passionate birth professionals! Jungian, Jean Shenoda Bolen said in her book, *The Millionth Circle,* "the only way to change ourselves, and the world, is to form a circle." Margaret Mead said, "Never doubt that a small group of thoughtful, committed citizens can change the world; indeed, it is the only thing that ever has."

Through all this wonderfulness, I must admit that recently, however, on a cold, dreary Saturday morning, that I found the idea of staying home by a warm fire, perhaps watching a sappy movie or two, more appealing than packing up and venturing out to teach a class. Of course, once I got there, I gave it my all, and was very happy to be there. At the end of the class, one of the expectant mothers came up to me and shared, "Now I can sleep tonight." I smiled, but clearly gave the look that says, "Perhaps you can explain that a little further." She continued by saying, "The past few weeks, I have not been able to sleep because I was worried and scared about how I was going to be able to give birth. Now, after taking and participating in your class, I have full confidence in my body, my partner, and the many comfort tools that we learned. So, I know I will sleep tonight since I am much calmer.

Thank you for making such a difference, and I know I can do this!" At moments like that, you do not know whether to hug or cry, so she, her partner, and I did both. Oh, did I mention that the calling of childbirth educator is a privilege and pleasure? The sappy movies by a warm fire can wait. The encouraged, motivated adult learners in the birth world cannot.

We are all unfinished, fascinating creatures. This is where and when the lifelong learning is such a phenomenal motivation to keep us curious and learning. Foster your own growth spurts. Stay that lifelong learner course for yourself and your students. You will sustain the flame of your passion through the ebb and flow of your life, your profession, and your actual teaching. Be cognizant of the impact you have made, and are making, to expectant families and the surrounding birth world. We all are leaves of the wisdom tree that flow with the seasons, yet continue to grow.

I sincerely hope that this book has, and will, reinforce and validate the wonderful contributions you are making to this life-altering field, and that it truly has added to your insights. Thank you for choosing and reading this labor of love, and continuing to be out there with your heart and knowledge making a difference.

For additional information and details in a variety of areas, especially using visuals and activities please read Connie's, *Innovative Teaching Strategies for Birth Professionals, Second Edition* by Connie Livingston, Praeclarus Press, 2015.

REFERENCES

Anderson, J. (2004). *A walk on the beach: Tales of wisdom from an unconventional woman.* New York: Broadway Books.

Bolen, J. S. (1999). *The millionth circle: How to change ourselves and the world: The essential guide to women's circles.* Berkeley, CA: Conari Press.

Brody, K. (2011). My body rocks. *Mothering Magazine, March/April,* 36-43.

Buckley, S. (2015). *Hormonal physiology of childbearing: Evidence and implications for women, babies and maternity care.* Retrieved from: Childbirth Connection. A program of the national partnership for women and families. http://www.nationalpartnership.org/research-library/maternal-health/hormonal-physiology-of-childbearing.pdf

Eastman-Mueller, H. et al. (2013). iRest (Integrative Restoration) Yoga Nidra on the College Campus: Changes in stress, depression, worry and mindfulness. *International Journal of Yoga Therapy, 23,* 15-24.

Jensen, J. (2004). *The development and impact of participatory behaviors on the andragogical learner: A manual for adult educators.* Doctoral dissertation.

Kim, S.D. (2014) Effects of yoga exercises of life stress and blood glucose levels in nursing students. *Journal of Physical Therapy Science, 26*(12), 2003-2006.

Roberts, L., Gulliver, B., Fisher, J., & Clyoes, K.G. (2010). The coping with labor algorithm: an alternative assessment tool for the laboring woman. *Journal of Midwifery Women's Health, 55,* 107-116.

Stankovic, L. (2011) Transforming trauma: a qualitative feasibility study of integrative restoration Yoga Nidra on combat-related post-traumatic stress disorder. *International Journal of Yoga Therapy, 21,* 23-37.

Women's Health Care Physicians. (n.d.). *Committee on obstetric practice: Oral intake during labor.* Retrieved from: http://www.acog.org/resources-And-Publications/Committee-Opinions/Committee-on-Obstetric-Practice/Oral-Intake-During-Labor

APPENDIX

This appendix includes samples of inserts included in the book. The class outlines for participant note-taking that were mentioned can also be available for a three-week series, a two-day Going Natural class, and a one-day Express class.

These are all attainable upon request for your use. Please contact me for any request, question, or comments.

Thank you again for being part of the journey,

Julie Jensen, PhD, LCCE, FACCE
juliejensen02@outlook.com

TEACHING IS...

- loving learning;
- giving yourself and your wisdom;
- empowering;
- humbling;
- learning from experience;
- not pretending to have all of the answers and/or solutions;
- having fun;
- letting go of control and not needing the power;
- being open to differing views;
- learning as much (probably more) from your students as they do from you;
- welcoming feedback;
- respecting your students;
- valuing each individual;
- developing your own style;
- encouraging students to develop their own as well;
- opening eyes and hearts, including your own;
- learning much about yourself;
- teaching half of what you know, which is still probably too much;
- learning your limits;
- learning to exceed your limits;
- realizing that...

"The truly successful teacher is the one
you will never need again."

— Ashleigh Brilliant

- ... and celebrating this.

"I have never let my schooling interfere with my education."

—Mark Twain

COMFORT STRATEGY REFERENCE LIST

Continuous Support: emotional, physical, flexible, knowledge of comfort strategies, encouraging, reminders

Knowledge of Labor and Birth Process
Awareness Options
Reframing Pain
Relaxation: down flow
Awareness of benefits: muscles, energy, alert, positive hormone production
Focal Point(s):   internal/external

Patterned breathing: deep, cleansing breaths
all slow and even
adapt during peak-faster or slower
preventing urge to push blow

Massage:
- downward (unless using counter pressure for back)
- neck, shoulder, arms
- palms
- upper and mid-back
- counter pressure for lower-back - upward thumbs, hands open or closed
  - one fist/ both fists, using knuckles
  - elbow/forearm, up or oval
  - use of massage tool(s)
  - racquet ball(s)
  - heat/cold

Double hip squeezes
Hydrotherapy
Receptors (physiological processes and evidence-based):
- palms–squeezing items, hand-holding, rolling tool
- soles–walking, standing, dancing/swaying, massage, sitting on ball, chair, couch, or bed
- pelvic floor–sitting on a firm, solid surface such as ball, chair, couch, tub, or bed
- lips–kissing, pointer finger, lip balm

Senses:
   Touch: massage, counter pressure, hugging, slow dancing,
               palms (holding hands, squeezing), soles, tub,
               shower

Pelvic floor:
   Smell: each other, own blanket, pillow and/or stuffed
               animal, lotion, oil
   Sight: partner, other support, lighting, setting environment
               with accessories, focal points, sentimental items
   Hearing: encouragement, music (relaxing, energizing, happy,
               dance) humming, moaning, singing, praying, quiet
   Taste: ice chips, small sips of clear liquid, popsicles,
               washcloth, lollipops

Position Changes/Movement:
   Upright: walking, swaying, dancing, standing, sitting/rocking,
               bar
   Leaning over: chair, couch, bed, partner

   Ball: bouncing/swaying
               leaning over
               back against wall
               sitting
   All fours
   Lunge
   Supported squat/squat dangle
   Shower/tub
   Side-lying

Dancing Examples: All can ignite the hip joint receptors, and
utilize pelvic movement and gravity
      Slow dancing- Support, rhythm, adding back massage
      Waltz- Moderate movement, intermittent opening of the pelvis
      Rumba- Pronounced hip movements and a somewhat faster pace
      Twist- Shoulder, back, hip, leg and foot movements and usually
               produces laughter

There are many other possibilities or you can make up your own.

PUSHING

Pushing can sometimes be as challenging to teach as it is to do!

STRATEGIES TO ASSIST MUSCLE AWARENESS AND DIFFERENTIATION FOR STAGE TWO PUSHING

- Focus on the vaginal opening/pelvic floor area through which the baby will pass; this will encourage the awareness to relax those muscles through the pressure and possible "ring of fire" sensation. Think "down and out," muscles and focus will follow.

- Encourage expectant moms to contract the muscles in the lower abdominal area to push down, as opposed to the facial muscles (purple pushing) or the rectal muscles, since the baby is not passing through either of those areas; make each pushing effort productive in the right direction.

- They can "find" those muscles by coughing and/or doing a deep, cleansing breath into the lower abdominal area; give them a chance to practice this; for further and more specific experience, they can do the "three-finger" pressure hold where they apply three fingers of one hand to the lower abdominal area to feel those muscles contract and push down. Once they master this, some can actually cause the three fingers to rise as they are resting on this area.

- Instruct expectant moms to push into the "ring of fire" and pelvic floor pressure when the time comes and they are actually pushing, not retract from it, to help relieve this sensation and to encourage further descent of the baby.

- To assist expectant moms to be aware of the location through which they are pushing, have them sit upright with their pelvic floor resting on their blanket or mat. Then have them do at least three slow kegel exercises, holding for a few seconds each time; after that, have them GENTLY bear down with their rectal muscles as if they are having a bowel movement. They then can either discuss their sensation awareness as a group or have them reflect individually with their partner on the location difference between these two sets of muscles.

Other ideas for teaching second stage:

_____

_____

_____

_____

_____

_____

_____

_____

_____

_____

_____

_____

ADULT LEARNING BILL OF RIGHTS
(AS TOLD BY THE ADULT LEARNER)

- Acknowledge my presence.
- Show interest in me as a learner.
- Look at me directly; acknowledge me as an individual within the group of learners.
- I need to know how much you care before I am aware of how much you know.
- Value my experience.
- Respect and praise the fact that I am seeking the information you have to offer.
- Seek my opinions though they may not coincide with yours.
- Hear, see, and feel what I am saying.
- Respect my time.
- Know that I am usually with you by choice.
- Honor my questions with honest answers.
- Value that I am asking questions.
- Be patient with me if I do not get it the first, second, or third time.
- Respect my previous learning.
- Assume not that because I am an adult that basic terms and ideas cannot be used.
- Honor my learning style and plan curriculum with the awareness that there are many styles.
- Provide me with independent problem-solving opportunities.
- Expect me to be self-directed.
- Do not be offended or hold it against me if I do not appear to be participating; I may be learning in a different way.

- Be prepared and organized for me to optimize my learning.

- Be specific with your expectations of me, whether it be in class, an assignment outside of class, and/or materials needed.

- Know that I am responsible for my own learning and participation.

- Seek my input regarding the rationale of the facts and methods that are offered.

- Avoid judgments of my appearance and attitudes.

- Be aware that I have adult responsibilities in my life.

- Have fun, enjoy, and appreciate what you are contributing to my life and yours.

TEACHING STRATEGIES

- Lecture: interactive, involving the group, such as feedback and asking them to finish your sentences.
- Needs Assessment
- Icebreakers
- Break-out Groups
- Handouts
- Models/Props
- Demonstration/Return Demonstration
- Interactive Discussion
- Question-Answer
- Video Clips
- PowerPoint
- Homework Assignments
- Scenario Cards
- Stories/Sharing
- Bags with Visuals (for points of presentation and discussion)
- Introductions– or other methods of sharing
- Setting the Environment: Music, Lighting, Arrangement, and Displays
- Validation (of concerns, questions, choices, beliefs)
- Wait Time
- Research (educator and/or participants)
- Tours
- Situational Practices
- Modeling
- Spiraling

EDUCATE YOURSELF AND OTHERS

Create your own environment

Omit concerns

Make yourself the expert

Movement

Unify your skills

Nullify the fear

Increase your confidence

Cooperate with your style

Align your thoughts

Take ownership

Invite your spirit

Obey your soul

Number your priorities

Trust in yourself

Recognize your skills

Understand yourself

Support yourself

Trust in your support

BIRTH POWER PLAN

Contractions:

_____

_____

_____

_____

_____

_____

Arrangements:

(pack, house, pets, pre-registration, insurance, baby items,
labor support)

_____

_____

_____

_____

_____

_____

Medications:

No _____

Yes _____

Maybe _____

Positions:

Other notes:

BALANCE AND RELAX!!

"Have you ever been too busy driving to stop for gas?"
- Stephen Covey

- Balance of the spirit, body, and soul is key.
- Take time for you!
- Clear the way– always keep the path to your heart open.
- Do for yourself more than what you would do for others!
- If you become your job, you lose you.
- There is power in balancing your lives and truly caring for yourself!
- Do what helps you to live a full life.
- Eliminate the stresses you have control over and add the comforts.
- Redefine your priorities, if that is what you need.
- Create time for yourself.

PROGRESSIVE RELAXATION FOR YOU

- Comfortable position and environment
- Deep cleansing breaths
- Self-body check: move down to follow the natural path of relaxation– top of head, face, neck, shoulders, arms, hands, back, chest, abdomen, bottom, thighs, calves, and feet
- One to five minutes daily minimum

ADDITIONAL ACTIVITIES FOR YOU

- Head rolls and front arm stretches with breaths
- Self-massage: temples, jaw line, shoulders, and feet
- Play
- Train massage
- Promise to yourself: small steps, not resolution!

Follow your promises and follow yourself. You are too important to be taken too seriously. While you are so serious with yourself, facts, others, etc., the soul train leaves the station without you!

Take care of yourself!

THE CONFIDENT EDUCATOR...

Opens the eyes and hearts of learners,
Is a life-long learner,
Values each individual,
Values each group,
Is open to differing viewpoints,
Welcomes feedback,
Learns from the students and their experiences,
Allows learning to happen for all.

"If we all did the things we are really capable of doing,
we would literally astound ourselves."
- Thomas Edison

What gifts do you have to make you a wonderful educator?

_____

_____

_____

_____

What might be challenging for you?

_____

_____

_____

_____

STYLES OF LEARNERS

LEARNING DOMAINS

These are the actions or thoughts applied to the approach of learning:

- Cognitive– understanding and application of ideas
- Affective– finding the relevant value with interest
- Psychomotor– action-oriented habitual learned response with some confidence and skill

LEARNING STYLES

- Auditory– listening, discussing, reading aloud
- Visual– taking notes, looking at instructions and illustrations, finding handouts helpful
- Kinesthetic– responding and learning with movement, having sense of balance and rhythm

How does your style of learning affect your teaching?

_____

_____

_____

_____

Name some specific characteristics that you can observe that will help you determine the learning styles of your participants.

_____

_____

_____

_____

Check off what Domains and Styles each of these activities meet:

ACTIVITY	LEARNING DOMAINS			LEARNING STYLES		
	Cognative	Affective	Psychomotor	Auditory	Visual	Kinesthetic
Introductions						
Floor practice-relaxation						
Lecture on Anatomy and Physiology						
Discussion on Birth Process using visuals						
Homework Research on Epidurals						
Role-play Labor Scenarios						
Hospital tour						
Labor stations						

POSSIBLE SCENARIOS FOR "POOP HAPPENS"

- We've been planning this baby for so long. We attended every prepared childbirth class, practiced every night, packed all of our labor tools and made arrangements for my best friend to take lots of pictures. Now I have to have a Cesarean delivery.

- It is now over. We had our baby. I guess everything is fine. I feel so lost being a mom and not pregnant anymore. I cannot believe it is really over-all that planning...

- I knew my birth would be beautiful. I would have skin-to-skin contact and breastfeed right away. But they had to take my baby to the nursery immediately.

- I had my baby so fast. We didn't get to use most of the techniques we practiced, the Personal Birth Plan we wrote, the labor tools, or the birth ball! Now it is over!

- I have been asked so many times about my biggest concern regarding parenting. There are probably so many I should have but I just do not know.

- I know I am supposed to feel much love for this baby... but she has a cone head, does not want to breastfeed, and does not seem to like even being held by me.

- I am not sure I know how to take care of this baby. Where do I learn?

- Why did I not get it when sooooo many people told us about sleep deprivation as new parents? I just need some sleep and for everyone to go home.

- My labor had to be induced. The doctor thought it would be better because of my blood pressure. It was so hard, I had to have an epidural–it only took on one side. The baby was in distress and so they had to do an episiotomy. Now he is under observation in the nursery. What happened to my natural childbirth I wanted to do? Sadly, this was a failure and so am I...

- I am going home today from the hospital without my baby. His nursery is all ready. We are supposed to have a family Baby Party on Sunday and I have no baby to take.

- Help! Why did no one tell me how hard this is? We wanted this beautiful baby in our lives. We have been home a week and this baby eats and poops more than he sleeps! I do not know what to do! I do not think I am a very good mom...

- Our baby was born with a pronounced birthmark on her cheek. Her grandparents want to know what happened to their granddaughter, like she is defective. What do I say?

WELCOME TO BIRTH ESSENTIALS!

Thank you for being here and being an important part of this class! You have made an important investment in your education, your birth experience, and your baby.

- Please be prompt and attend every class.
- Plan on bringing your book to every class and do your outside reading.
- Bring your pillows, blankets, drinks, and snacks to every class.
- Please feel free to ask questions.
- Participate to your comfort level and have fun!

Julie Jensen, PhD, LCCE, FACCE
Lamaze® Certified Childbirth Educator

CLASS ONE

Welcome, Class Policies, Handouts, Sharing
Prepared Childbirth and Labor Tools
Pain Management

Break

Anatomy & Physiology of Pregnancy and Birth
Discomforts & Warning Signs
Nutrition in the Third Trimester
Contractions
Signs of Labor
Early Labor
Induction

Break

Floor Practice
    Active Relaxation and Comfort Techniques
    Slow-Paced Breathing (First Level)

Closure & Review

CONTRACTIONS: **POSSIBLE SIGNS OF LABOR** **WHEN TO CALL:**

CONTRACTIONS:	POSSIBLE SIGNS OF LABOR	WHEN TO CALL:
1.	1.	1.
2.	2.	2.
3.	3.	3.
4.	4.	4.

WHAT TO DO: 5.   **ASSIGNMENTS:**

WHAT TO DO:	5.	ASSIGNMENTS:
1.	6.	1.
2.		2.
3.		3.
4.		4.

PRACTICE PLAN:

CLASS TWO

Review, Questions, Handouts, Sharing
Fetal Monitoring
Active Labor
Pain Medication Options
Transition Phase of Labor
Childbirth Videos

Break

Receptors and Tools
Floor Practice
    Review Active Relaxation, Comfort Techniques and
      Slow-Paced Breathing
    Laboring and Comfort Positions
    Modified – Paced Breathing (Second Level)
    Patterned – Paced Breathing (Third Level)
    Possible Challenges in Labor

Closure & Review

Receptors:	**Assignments**
_____	1. _____
_____	2. _____
_____	3. _____
_____	4. _____
_____	5. _____
_____	
_____	
_____	
_____	
_____	
_____	

PRACTICE PLAN:

CLASS THREE

Tour
Review, Questions, Handouts, Sharing
Presentation and Position of Baby
Pelvic Station
Back Labor
Second Stage—Pushing and Delivery

Break

Floor Practice
    Relaxation Review
    Review of Breathing Patterns and Possible Challenges
    Review of Comfort Techniques
    Pushing Techniques

Closure and Review

Coping Strategies for Labor:	**Assignments:**
1. _____	1. _____
2. _____	2. _____
3. _____	3. _____
4. _____	4. _____
5. _____	
6. _____	
7. _____	
8. _____	

PRACTICE PLAN:

GOING NATURAL BIRTH CLASS

Thank you for being here and being an important part of this class! You have made an important investment in your education, your birth experience and your baby.

- Please be prompt and attend every class.
- Plan on bringing your book to every class and do your outside reading.
- Bring your pillows, blankets, drinks, and snacks to every class.
- Please feel free to ask questions.
- Participate to your comfort level and have fun!

Julie Jensen, PhD, LCCE, FACCE
Lamaze® Certified Childbirth Educator

CLASS SERIES OUTLINE

CLASS ONE
Welcome, Class Policies, Handouts, Sharing
Prepared Childbirth and Labor Tools
The Normal, Natural Process of Birth
Anatomy & Physiology of Birth
Stages and Phases of Birth
Contractions
Signs of Labor, What To Do
Comfort Strategies and Their Benefits
Confidence, Empowerment, Knowledge of Options
Active Relaxation, Support, Environment
Massage, Breathing, Positions, Ball
Closure & Review

CONTRACTIONS: **POSSIBLE SIGNS OF LABOR**   **WHEN TO CALL:**

1._____   1._____   1._____
2._____   2._____   2._____
3._____   3._____   3._____
4._____   4._____   4._____

WHAT TO DO: 5._____   **ASSIGNMENTS:**

1._____   6._____   1._____
2._____   2._____
3._____   3._____
4._____   4._____

REVIEW

_____
_____
_____
_____
_____
_____
_____

PRACTICE PLAN:

_____
_____
_____
_____
_____
_____
_____
_____

CLASS TWO

Review, Questions, Handouts, Sharing
Presentation and Position of Baby
Back Labor
What If...Introduction, Medications, Cesarean Birth
Pain In Labor and Receptors
Using Your Own Body's Capabilities
Putting It All Together
Review Active Relaxation and Comfort Strategies
Relaxation, Massage, Breathing, Positions
Possible Challenges in Labor
Pushing Techniques
Birth Plan
Review and Closure

Receptors:

_____

_____

_____

_____

_____

_____

_____

_____

_____

_____

_____

_____

Coping Strategies for Labor:

1. _____
2. _____
3. _____
4. _____
5. _____
6. _____
7. _____
8. _____

Birth Plan:

C _____
A. _____
M _____
P _____

PRACTICE PLAN:

_____
_____
_____
_____
_____
_____
_____
_____
_____
_____
_____
_____
_____
_____
_____

EXPRESS CLASS OUTLINE

Welcome, Handouts, Sharing
Labor Tools and Pain Management
Anatomy & Physiology of Pregnancy and Birth
Contractions
Early, Active, and Transition Phases of Labor – First Stage
Birth Options DVD
Presentation and Position of Baby
Pushing and Delivery – Second Stage
Third and Fourth Stages/Postpartum
Comfort Techniques/Labor Rehearsal:
    Active Relaxation
    Breathing Patterns and other comfort tools
    Pushing Techniques
    Closing

CONTRACTIONS:
1._____
2._____
3._____
4._____

WHAT TO DO:
1._____
2._____
3._____
4._____

POSSIBLE SIGNS OF LABOR
1._____
2._____
3._____
4._____
5._____
6._____

WHEN TO CALL:
1._____
2._____
3._____
4._____

ASSIGNMENTS:
1._____
2._____
3._____
4._____

Coping Strategies for Labor:
1. _____
2. _____
3. _____
4. _____
5. _____
6. _____
7. _____
8. _____

Assignments:
1. _____
2. _____
3. _____
4. _____

PRACTICE PLAN:

EXAMPLES OF APPROPRIATE ACTION VERBS

OR MEASURABLE TERMS THAT COULD BE USED TO CONSTRUCT MEASURABLE OBJECTIVES

- Recognize
- Compare
- Identify
- Describe
- Demonstrate
- Discuss
- Contrast
- Develop
- Construct
- State
- List
- Define
- Summarize
- Give Examples of
- Explain

ABOUT THE AUTHORS

 Julie Jensen has been in the childbirth education and adult learning fields for over three decades. She has a bachelor's degree in clinical and physiological psychology and a PhD in participatory adult learning that has become a manual for adult educators. She has written curricula for and taught a number of childbirth preparation and other prenatal classes including traditional, natural, adolescent, expectant fathers and antepartum needs. She is also a registered psychotherapist in Colorado, and is currently a Parent Education Coordinator and childbirth educator in a hospital setting. *The Dance of Teaching Childbirth Education* is her first book.

 Connie Livingston was a birth researcher, journalist, and childbirth educator, and founder of Perinatal Education Associates, Inc. She was a frequent speaker at birth conferences, and taught doula and childbirth educator training workshops. In 2013, Connie became the International Childbirth Education Association (ICEA) President-Elect, and in 2015, assumed the role as President of ICEA. Connie Livingston passed away on December 29th, 2016, at the age of 60. She is survived by her daughters Heather Livingston and Erin Livingston.

More books from Praeclarus Press

Under One Sky: Intimate Encounters with Moms and Babies by a Breastfeeding Consultant and Nurse

Chris Auer

Under One Sky recounts poignant encounters surrounding birth, breastfeeding, and the life circumstances of families from over 77 countries. As a lactation consultant, Chris Auer met with thousands of women as they began their mothering and breastfeeding journey, women from places as diverse as The Congo, Ecuador, Italy, and Nepal, as well as American women from all walks of life. The babies range from healthy, full-term to extremely premature. The mothers range from 12 to 52. Chris Auer has worked passionately to champion mothers on this segment of their life journey. In the retelling of their stories, we see the importance of meeting mothers where they are in the moment, with an accepting, listening presence. *Under One Sky* is beyond a memoir; it's a mosaic of their stories and reveals a poignant picture of our connectedness.

Battling Over Birth: Black Women and the Maternal Health Care Crisis

Julia Chinyere Oparah

"*Battling over Birth* is a critical and timely resource for understanding black women's birthing experiences in the United States, a country where black women's lives—and the lives they create—are at much greater risk of death and injury than those of non-black women ... By distilling the common and diverse threads from over 100 black women, the Black Women Birthing Justice researchers have woven a multi-faceted tapestry that reflects what black women view as important and central to optimal birth experiences. Their recommendations for improving care and outcomes are grounded in black women's authoritative knowledge. ... This wonderful, important, necessary research by and for black women points in the direction that black women think we should go to ensure they have safe, healthy, and satisfying birth experiences and outcomes. We need to listen and act."

—Christine Morton, PhD, author, *Birth Ambassadors: Doulas and the Re-Emergence of Woman-Supported Birth in America*

Made in the USA
Monee, IL
14 June 2024

59965779R00115